Rapture or Tribulation

by Susan Davis

© Copyright 2013 – Susan Davis

ISBN-13: 978-1482600629

ISBN-10: 1482600625

NOTICE: You are encouraged to distribute copies of this document through any means, electronic or in printed form. You may post this material, in whole or in part, on your website or anywhere else. But we do request that you include this notice so others may know they can copy and distribute as well. This book is available as a free ebook and mp3 at the website:

http://end-times-prophecy.com

© 2013 by Susan Davis

Unless indicated otherwise, all Scripture reference and notes are from the King James Version Bible.

TABLE OF CONTENTS

1. Do Not Be So Sure Of Yourself   6

2. A Partial Surrender Leads To Death   13

3. The Hour Of My Return Is Closing In   22

4. Do Not Despair In These Dark Days   25

5. I Take No Pleasure In Punishing Men   29

6. It Will Be Just As The Days Of Noah And Lot   35

7. This Is Your Purpose For Living: To Choose "For" Or "Against" God   39

8. I Want A Pure Bride   44

9. Come Away From The Path Of Destruction You Are On   48

10. So Few Are Listening   68

11. I Cannot Take You If You ... Ignore MY Instructions   72

12. Don't Be Like Lot's Wife   77

13. Children, Seek Me In All Things   84

14. Nothing Can Stop What I Have Ordained — 91

15. Take Off Your Blinders – Open Your Eyes — 105

16. They Devise A God In Their Own Mind — 109

17. Very Few Are Watching Or Waiting On Me — 112

18. Don't Spend Another Moment Outside Of My Precious Will — 124

19. My Kingdom Will Consist Of Those … Few Who Have Found Me To Be Worthy Of Their Utmost Devotion — 127

20. Stop Struggling, Looking For That Which Can Only Be Found In Me — 135

21. I Am Looking Forward To Meeting With You — 146

22. I Will Not Allow This World To Carry On Much Longer — 153

23. Repent Of Your Evil: Your Wicked Plans Of Making Goals And A Future Apart From Your God — 156

24. I Can Bring You From Whatever Sin You Have Been Engaging In — 171

ABOUT THESE PROPHECIES

Susan operates in the gift of prophecy. In 1 Corinthians 14:1 it states, "Follow the way of love and eagerly desire gifts of the Spirit, especially prophecy." Now we are living and supposed to be obeying God's instructions in the New Testament. Although some believe that spiritual gifts, such as prophecies, have been done away with, this is man's thinking and not God's. God has not changed His covenant. We are still living in the era of the New Covenant – which is also called the New Testament. Please understand that your first commitment should be to the Lord Jesus Christ and His Word as written in the Bible – especially the New Testament.

As always, all prophecy needs to be tested against the Bible. However, if the prophecy lines up with the Bible then we are expected to obey it. Currently God does not use prophecies to introduce new doctrines. They are used to reinforce what God has already given to us in the Bible. God also uses them to give us individual warnings of future events that will affect us.

Just like in the Old Testament, God uses prophets in the New Testament times of which we are currently in. The book of Acts, which is in the New Testament, mentions some of the prophets such as Judas and Silas (Acts 15:32) and Agabus (Acts 21:21) and there were others. The ministry of prophets is also mentioned in New Testament times in 1 Corinthians 12:28, 14:1,29,32,37 as well as in Ephesians 2:20,3:5,4:11.

Jesus chooses prophets to work for Him on earth. Among other things, Jesus uses prophecies and prophets to communicate His desires to His children. The Bible itself was written prophetically through the inspiration of the Holy Spirit.

Some people say words of prophecy are in danger of adding to the Bible or taking from it -- well the Bible speaks of prophecy as being a Gift of the HOLY SPIRIT. The way the Bible is added to or taken from is not through additional words of prophecy received by the people which the HOLY SPIRIT gives words to, but by the changing of GOD's concepts to add new unBiblical concepts from other pagan beliefs for example. But the primary work of the prophets in the Bible has always been to focus the people back to GOD's WORD, the BIBLE.

As it says in 1 Thessalonians 5:19-21, "Do not put out the Spirit's fire; do not treat prophecies with contempt. Test everything. Hold on to the good." And the way to test the messages is to compare it's content to what the Bible says.

In all the prophecies below I personally (Mike Peralta - Book Preparer) have tested these messages and they are all in agreement to what the Bible says. But you must also test these messages, yourself, to the Bible. And if they are consistent with the Bible, then God expects that you will take them to heart and obey His instructions.

1. Do Not Be So Sure Of Yourself

The LORD's Words for Today (Posted at www.End-Times-Prophecy.Com)

"This life is only a stepping stone to the next life..."

(The LORD gave this Word to Susan on May 3, 2012)

Daughter, take down MY Words:

Children these Words are for you:

The hour is closing in for MY Return. So few are paying attention...so few seek ME...so few even open MY Book. There are great losses coming for those who disregard ME, for those who choose not to pursue ME, and for those who refuse to acknowledge ME—I am the Great GOD of the Universe—I created it all—I put the stars in place. I established the firmament of the earth. I blew the Breath of Life into every living creature—it is MY Breath that sustains you—you live because I deem it so.

I give and I take away. Do not be so sure of yourself. You do not own tomorrow. All can change in a moment's notice. Many who are sure of themselves have been proved wrong when they come before ME—why take chances with your eternal salvation and your eternal destination?

This life is only a stepping stone to the next life, so what direction will you move in—toward ME and eternal life abundant or toward MY enemy to life apart from your MAKER toward eternal damnation, hell, and suffering? This should be an easy choice, but so few make the right choice as the road to hell is broad, but the road to eternal salvation is narrow and few find it.

Be wise and spend this time I have given you wisely. Seek ME, Seek MY Ways. There is no better path to take. All other paths lead to destruction.

I grow weary of MY children refusing to heed MY Words. I tire of seeing MY children fall away, so many are lost into the hands of MY enemy. It is disheartening children, when I make MY Blood so available. I paid the price. Your ransom has been paid. I did it with MY OWN Blood spilt.

Now it is up to you to claim this gift and to come under this blood covering that will bring you freedom, salvation, and safe passage into MY Kingdom for eternity. Why let such a great gift get by you? You have but to surrender your all to ME, repent from a remorseful heart for your sins, lay your life before ME. Make ME your LORD and Master. I will save you from the penalty of your sin: hell and torment everlasting.

Let ME Save you, let ME Free you. Put ME at the center of your life and let ME fill you with MY Precious HOLY SPIRIT. We will walk with you through this life and for eternity and make our home with you. The future can be bright; your days can be spent with ME for eternity. I am the ONE WHO created you and I know you better than you know yourself. Why choose to spend eternity apart from ME?

This hour before you is short, as the world will soon be ruled By MY enemy and I will place MY beloved bride away to safety from the evil that is about to consume the earth: so few are coming when I call out MY bride. You do not need to suffer under the tyranny of MY enemy. Give ME a full surrender of your life and come to ME with a repentant heart. This is what I require.

You do not need to fear the future. I will bring you peace of mind. There is no other way to safety.

Choose this day who you will serve.

The LORD GOD JEHOVAH.

MAKER of the Things Above and the Things Below

Joshua 2:11: And as soon as we had heard these things, our hearts did melt, neither did there remain any more courage in any man, because of you: for the LORD your GOD, HE is GOD in heaven above, and in earth beneath.

Genesis 1:16: And GOD made two great lights; the greater light to rule the day, and the lesser light to rule the night: HE made the stars also.

Genesis 1:7-9: ⁷ And GOD made the firmament, and divided the waters which were under the firmament from the waters which were above the firmament: and it was so. ⁸ And GOD called the firmament Heaven. And the evening and the morning were the second day.

Matthew 7:14: Because strait is the gate, and narrow is the way, which leadeth unto life, and few there be that find it.

Joshua 24:15: And if it seem evil unto you to serve the LORD, choose you this day whom ye will serve; whether the gods which your fathers served that were on the other side of the flood, or the gods of the Amorites, in whose land ye dwell: but as for me and my house, we will serve the LORD.

Genesis 49:25: Even by the GOD of thy father, WHO shall help thee; and by the ALMIGHTY, WHO shall bless thee with blessings of heaven above, blessings of the deep that lieth under, blessings of the breasts, and of the womb:

If You Cling To The World, You Cling To Death

(Letter Dictated by the LORD to Susan, May 8, 2012)

Children, this is your LORD Speaking. Many wonder about the timing of MY Coming. Children the hour is approaching swiftly. I know you doubt this Word. I have spoken through many people; through many signs and wonders; through visions and dreams; through old and young alike.

You have been well forewarned. You will stand without excuse when I come for MY children, if you remain behind because of your doubt and unbelief. I have provided many Words through many people. Those who will listen are already seeking. Those who choose not to listen are already enthralled with this world, this evil, corrupt world.

Why MY children press into this world and not to their LORD and SAVIOR, their CREATOR, REDEEMER is only due to selfish pursuits and self will and unwillingness to love the LORD GOD with all your heart, soul, mind, and strength.

Children, I want you to listen closely: I am a GOD you can trust. You can follow ME and trust ME completely. When I say I am coming and to look for ME when certain specific things come to pass, you know this Word can be trusted. MY Word is consistent, reliable, solid. I do not change. What I say I will do, I DO! I do not flinch. I cannot be moved. I will come and rescue MY bride. Will you be among her? Will you die to self and surrender your life over to ME completely? If you do not do this, then as MY Word says, I cannot take you with ME.

To be made ready for MY Kingdom, I must see in your heart remorse for your sin past and a desire to give ME your life: a full surrender—although you do not know what this means, you must be willing to trust ME.

The hour approaches for MY Soon Return. The earth has turned grossly against ME embracing MY enemy and his ways. Few really seek the path of holiness: the separation from the world I require of MY bride. The world is too tantalizing. It offers only death but few see the disguise of MY enemy who comes as an angel of light. Few want to believe MY Words that I require separation from the love of the world and her ways. She walks apart from MY Will and moves aggressively against MY Ways, MY Precious Ways.

Children, I have given you many signs to look for. You know what to look for. MY Words are true. It is no accident that you see many things spoken of in MY Word now coming to pass. Only those who care not to see, who refuse to believe—they cannot see what lies before them. I cannot help you if you do not read MY Book and seek ME for all truth. Only with a full surrender, repentance of sin, and a complete filling of MY HOLY SPIRIT will the scales fall off your spiritual eyes so that MY Word, MY Truth will come to life for you.

If you cling to the world, you cling to death. This world is dying and the more it pulls away from ME, its GOD, the more death will come upon her and those who inhabit her. Make yourself ready to depart when I come for MY bride, MY true church. This is the only way to life. Embrace the world and die. She is an enmity to ME.

Come in close. Get to know ME.

I am the GOD JEHOVAH...

ALMIGHTY...

EVERLASTING...

SONG of the saints.

Children, put your love for the world aside. Come to know what true love means in and through ME.

Your LORD and SAVIOR,

GOD MOST HIGH.

Matthew 24:6-8: [6] And ye shall hear of wars and rumours of wars: see that ye be not troubled: for all these things must come to pass, but the end is not yet. [7] For nation shall rise against nation, and kingdom against kingdom: and there shall be famines, and pestilences, and earthquakes, in divers places. [8] All these are the beginning of sorrows.

Mark 13:28-37: [28] Now learn a parable of the fig tree; When her branch is yet tender, and putteth forth leaves, ye know that summer is near: [29] So ye in like manner, when ye shall see these things come to pass, know that it is nigh, even at the doors. [30] Verily I say unto you, that this generation shall not pass, till all these things be done. [31] Heaven and earth shall pass away: but my words shall not pass away. [32] But of that day and that hour knoweth no man, no, not the angels which are in heaven, neither the SON, but the FATHER. [33] Take ye heed, watch and pray: for ye know not when the time is. [34] For the SON of Man is as a man taking a far journey, who left his house, and gave authority to his servants, and to every man his work, and commanded the porter to watch. [35] Watch ye therefore:

for ye know not when the master of the house cometh, at even, or at midnight, or at the cockcrowing, or in the morning: ³⁶ Lest coming suddenly he find you sleeping. ³⁷ And what I say unto you I say unto all, Watch.

James 4:4: Ye adulterers and adulteresses, know ye not that the friendship of the world is enmity with GOD? Whosoever therefore will be a friend of the world is the enemy of GOD.

John 12:25: He that loveth his life shall lose it; and he that hateth his life in this world shall keep it unto life eternal.

John 15:19: If ye were of the world, the world would love his own: but because ye are not of the world, but I have chosen you out of the world, therefore the world hateth you.

1 John 2:15: Love not the world, neither the things that are in the world. If any man loves the world, the love of the FATHER is not in him.

Deuteronomy 30:9-10: ⁹ And the LORD thy GOD will make thee plenteous in every work of thine hand, in the fruit of thy body, and in the fruit of thy cattle, and in the fruit of thy land, for good: for the LORD will again rejoice over thee for good, as HE rejoiced over thy fathers:¹⁰ If thou shalt hearken unto the Voice of the LORD thy GOD, to keep HIS Commandments and HIS Statutes which are written in this Book of the Law, and if thou turn unto the LORD thy GOD with all thine heart, and with all thy soul.

2. A Partial Surrender Leads To Death

Words Received from Our LORD by Susan, May 4, 2012

Only I give the Power you need to keep you in MY Will. The flesh cannot succeed at staying in the Will of GOD. Only by MY Power is any man successful in walking in MY Will—flesh cannot accomplish this task. It is the Power of the HOLY SPIRIT.

A partial surrender does not allot the fullness of MY SPIRIT to bring the individual under the controlling Power of MY SPIRIT thus they cannot successfully ward off evil, sin, and be in MY Will. They are considered "lukewarm" and lost. Partial surrender is not "surrender." Make no mistake; a partial surrender leads to death the same as an outright denial of ME as GOD.

Repentance is "key" to the person's surrender. If they are still believing they have no sin or they don't need forgiveness how can they be freed by the evil that still controls them?

Remorse over sin is the beginning of healing—healing heart, soul, spirit—all is interrelated. A repentant heart, a humble heart, can receive the salvation of their soul and will enter MY Kingdom upon receiving the HOLY SPIRIT by baptism.

This is part of releasing the person into freedom to be freed of demonic spirits: true remorse over past sin, acknowledgement of sin before a HOLY GOD and then the filling of MY SPIRIT and total submission to MY Ways and to ME as the individual's LORD and MASTER.

All other expressions are weak and ineffectual. The person must be submitted to ME completely to be relieved of the power of MY enemy and I must be their undisputed MASTER so that the individual can be walking in MY Will conquering sin and filled with the Power of MY SPIRIT. Not before will the individual be able to deal successfully with vanquishing sin in their lives. This is the "narrow path." All other paths lead to destruction.

Deuteronomy 30:19: I call heaven and earth to record this day against you, that I have set before you life and death, blessing and cursing: therefore choose life, that both thou and thy seed may live:

MY children, this is your LORD Speaking. I am coming very soon. MY Coming is near, even at the door. I am coming! You need to make ready.

This journal was completed during a 40-day fast by MY daughter Susan. She did this fast at MY Request. I brought her to a secluded location so that she might die to herself. During this time, I gave her many Words that I wanted to go out to MY children. So she wrote MY Words as I led her. All these Letters have important information you need to read and consider, as MY Coming is near.

This is your LORD and SAVIOR, YAHUSHU.

May 20, 2012

The LORD's Words for Today (Posted at www.End-Times-Prophecy.Com)

Dear Faithful Followers of CHRIST:

In this letter are many important things to note: three End Times warning letters from our LORD; important weekly updates of the young boys Jonathan and Sebastian's dreams and visions and Buddy Baker's newest end times vision; announcement for our FREE upcoming End Times Conference; info about our End Times

News Reports; and announcement of the "Marriage Supper of the LAMB" Ebook with important Words from our LORD. GOD bless you!

Come Out Of The Harlot Churches

(Word received from the LORD by Susan, May 14, 2011)

Listen to MY Words and I will direct your writing:

Children, it is I, your LORD. There is much I need to impart on you. The world has turned against ME wholesale. They have sold themselves to the devil. It is a frightening time for the people of this earth. I am lifting MY Hand of protection off of these people. For they consider ME not. They have chosen against ME, so I must leave them to their own devises. I must let them struggle in their own sin. Soon they will find out the meaning of turning away from a Holy GOD toward other sources of aid.

MY children, when you reach out to the world as your source of security you will learn you are only grasping at empty air. You are entrusting your life to MY enemy. He has plans for your life and none of it good as he comes to steal, kill, destroy.

Children, I offer relief to the uncertain future you fear. I am the CERTAIN. I am the RELIABLE. I can be trusted. I can save you from this world that is collapsing. MY children, as the world continues on its downward spiral of evil, there is hope through ME. I am the SAFE PATH, the SAFE ROUTE.

Come to ME in humble submission. Give ME your heart, your life. Let ME fill you with MY SPIRIT. There is no other answer. There is no other way.

Repent for your sin of pursuing the world and its ways and seeking after mammon and the traditions of men for your answers. Remove yourself from the harlot church that refuses to follow MY SPIRIT. Run from the churches who block the way for the move of MY SPIRIT.

Those that block MY SPIRIT and keep HIM at bay are nothing less than wolves in sheep's clothing and the price they will pay for destroying MY Work will be eternal condemnation.

Come out of the harlot churches, MY children! Come out from the cold and lukewarm! Come away from the dead churches! Seek ME in all MY Fullness. You cannot fight the enemy without a full oil lamp. You cannot even see him.

Fill your lamp and let ME give you new eyes to see MY Word more clearly, to be bold in spreading MY Word, to come to ME in humble repentance, to follow the one and only true path—the narrow road. Only those who have escaped the ways of the lukewarm will be ready when I return for MY church.

I am coming for a church that is filled with MY HOLY SPIRIT Fire and not the cold and dying church that loves ME not.

O' church of the living dead: come to ME before this great hour of disaster is upon you. Break free of your bondage to the traditions of men and the workings of the devil. He has you securely in his grip. You are greatly deceived. Take your blinders off and turn to ME for eye salve so that I might show you Truth.

The hour is short. This world is dying. Soon I will return to remove MY church, those who love ME more than the world. Turn to ME before it is too late. Turn while you are still able. Evil man is rising.

Don't be caught unawares. MY Warnings are sure and MY Word is True.

I am a GOD WHO does not lie. MY Word is coming to pass, just as I said it would. Read MY Word. See that I am a GOD WHO is true to HIS Word.

FAITHFUL FRIEND WHO sticks closer than a brother,

LORD GOD ALMIGHTY.

John 10:10: The thief cometh not, but for to steal, and to kill, and to destroy: I am come that they might have life, and that they might have it more abundantly.

Job 8:13-14: [13]So are the paths of all that forget GOD; and the hypocrite's hope shall perish: [14]whose hope shall be cut off, and whose trust shall be a spider's web.

Psalm 16:11: THOU wilt shew me the path of life: in THY Presence is fullness of joy; at THY Right Hand there are pleasures for evermore.

Matthew 25:3-4: [3] They that were foolish took their lamps, and took no oil with them: [4] But the wise took oil in their vessels with their lamps.

Matthew 6:24: No man can serve two masters: for either he will hate the one, and love the other; or else he will hold to the one, and despise the other. Ye cannot serve GOD and mammon.

Matthew 7:15: Beware of false prophets, which come to you in sheep's clothing, but inwardly they are ravening wolves.

Proverbs 18:24: A man that hath friends must shew himself friendly: and there is a friend that sticketh closer than a brother.

Getting To Know Me And My Ways - This Is The Meaning Of Life

Word of the LORD:

"You have two directions—only two—you either follow ME fully or you go with MY enemy..."

(Word received from the LORD by Susan, May 14, 2012)

Listen closely as I give you Words:

Daughter, I am coming and MY Time to collect MY children is drawing near: so many do not know ME, so many do not even care to know ME.

I am a GOD worth knowing. I created each child. I have put forth great effort in the creation of MY children. All MY children I love as only a father would love his own. Too many believe otherwise, that I am distant, far off, and aloof. This is not the case at all. I am really quite accessible, if only people would pursue ME. If only they would seek MY Face. Get close, come to know ME—really know ME.

There is nothing greater and more important than knowing GOD and getting to know ME and MY Ways. This is the meaning of life. All other pursuits are meaningless and out of the Will of GOD: the Will of the ONE WHO Created you.

Why walk outside of the Will of your CREATOR for your life? Your self will apart from MY Will is the will of the devil. Yes, it is your freewill to choose to walk the broad road and not the narrow way. You walk hand-in-hand with the devil whether you realize it or not.

To be out of MY Will is to be in the enemy's will and that is playing with fire and will lead to your ultimate destruction. To be completely and securely in MY Will you must surrender your all to ME, repent of your sins from a remorseful heart. Let ME fill you with MY SPIRIT. Allow ME to come into your life and bring you to a complete filling of MY SPIRIT, a full oil lamp. There is no other way.

You may seek after other routes, but only one leads to MY FATHER and that is through ME, the LORD and SAVIOR of mankind. All other paths lead to destruction.

Children, I am a GOD WHO is humble. I was willing to lay down MY Life for you in a humbling fashion to surrender all for your sin, to cover your price, to ransom you, to defeat the hold of MY enemy on your life, to release you from eternal bondage, torment, and destruction in hell.

You have two directions—only two—you either follow ME fully or you go with MY enemy and he is your father, the father of lies. Until you lay your life at MY Feet—you belong to the devil.

When MY children spend time with ME but refuse to give ME their all in a full surrender, they are still engaging with MY enemy. You cannot come into MY Kingdom unless you turn your life over to ME fully.

I am a Jealous GOD. I do not share with other gods. Either MY children belong to ME from a full surrender and pursue ME in their hearts daily or they belong to the devil, their god. He rules their heart and they are far from ME acting in the will of the one they have chosen. They worship the devil and his ways when they are outside MY Will.

There is no middle ground or halfway. MY children are either surrendered fully or they are not part of ME: MY SPIRIT does not move through them and they work against MY Kingdom and do the will of MY enemy. This is pure evil; although few see it and few find the narrow path into MY Kingdom.

There is only a small remnant who will come with ME out of the earth when I call MY church home. Only those who submit to MY Will fully, only those who willingly lay down their lives and step off the broad road of the ways of the world and MY enemy. Few are willing to do this. Therefore few will inherit the Kingdom of heaven. Read MY Book. I have made this point clear.

You cannot alter the Words in MY book. MY Truth stands. Few find the narrow path. Do you wish to be one of them? Come lay your life at MY Feet. Let ME use it to reach others. Allow ME access to your life so that I can fill you with MY SPIRIT, make you complete and lead you to tranquility and peace, the peace that passes all understanding. This is the purpose of your life: to love and serve ME, your CREATOR and to be made whole and complete through the filling of MY SPIRIT.

Let ME bear your burdens. Your life was not meant to be lived in fear. Cast your cares on ME. Make ME your GOD, worship ME, and I will deliver you out to safety.

The hour is short; you have precious little time left. Don't choose against ME.

I know you. I created you. Don't separate yourself from ME for eternity.

I am your Loving FATHER,

RULER of Heaven and Earth.

ETERNAL "I AM"

Psalm 42:1: As the hart panteth after the water brooks, so panteth my soul after THEE, O GOD.

Matthew 7:13: Enter ye in at the strait gate: for wide is the gate, and broad is the way, that leadeth to destruction, and many there be which go in thereat:

Matthew 7:21: Not everyone that saith unto ME, LORD, LORD, shall enter into the Kingdom of heaven; but he that doeth the Will of my FATHER which is in heaven.

John 8:44: Ye are of your father the devil, and the lusts of your father ye will do. He was a murderer from the beginning, and abode not in the truth, because there is no truth in him. When he speaketh a lie, he speaketh of his own: for he is a liar, and the father of it.

Mark 10:45: For even the SON of man came not to be ministered unto, but to minister, and to give HIS Life a ransom for many.

Matthew 7:14: Because strait is the gate, and narrow is the way, which leadeth unto life, and few there be that find it.

Exodus 15:11: Who is like unto THEE, O LORD, among the gods? Who is like THEE, glorious in holiness, fearful in praises, doing wonders?

3. The Hour Of My Return Is Closing In

Word of the LORD:

"All that I promised to happen in MY Book are coming together before your very eyes..."

(Words given by the LORD to Susan, May 17, 2012)

Listen carefully as I am about to give you new Words:

Children listen to ME. This is your LORD.

The hour of MY Return is closing in. If you are watching you already know this. MY children, you cannot deny that the world has become dark and evil. All are turning their backs to ME in unison. Only MY remnant bride remains untouched. She is small in number—very few pursue ME on the level I require; all others hunger after the world. The world holds them too tightly in its grip.

Soon, I will put aside the few who really seek ME and I will leave the rest to face MY Wrath and the vengeance of MY enemy. Mankind will suffer in this, the last hour. These days are about to come to fruition. I am giving you ample warning. I am supplying you with an abundance of signs and messages from those I have sent ahead to warn.

MY Words and MY Warnings have been clear, so many choose not to regard them. Very few seem to be alarmed by what is coming to this earth. Already the affects are being seen from the lifting of MY Hand of protection over the earth.

Children, come to your senses. Look around. See that MY Warnings and Messages are coming to pass and all that I promised to happen in MY Book are coming together before your very eyes.

Pull off your blinders. Look around. Read MY Book. Seek ME through humility and prayer. I will show you Truth and lead you down MY Safe Path. All other paths are marked for death. Leave the world behind. Seek ME for Truth and Safety. Humble yourself. Repent of your sins. Surrender your life completely to ME. I will save you. I am willing.

You cannot save yourself. No one can save you but ME. It is MY Blood spilt on Calvary that has paid your ransom for a lifetime of sin against a Holy GOD. Let ME secure your future with ME for eternity. Come with ME when I retrieve MY bride.

I am ready. Are you? Are you coming out to safety? Ask yourself and get right with your GOD. The hour is slipping away.

Your KING, REDEEMER, RESCUER,

"ADONAI"

Luke 21:11: And great earthquakes shall be in diverse places, and famines, and pestilences; and fearful sights and great signs shall there be from heaven.

1 John 2:15: Love not the world, neither the things that are in the world. If any man loves the world, the love of the FATHER is not in him.

Philippians 2:15: That ye may be blameless and harmless, the sons of GOD, without rebuke, in the midst of a crooked and perverse nation, among whom ye shine as lights in the world;

Matthew 20:16: So the last shall be first, and the first last: for many be called, but few chosen.

Acts 20:28: Take heed therefore unto yourselves, and to all the flock, over the which the HOLY GHOST hath made you overseers, to feed the church of GOD, which HE hath purchased with HIS Own Blood.

Hebrews 9:12: Neither by the blood of goats and calves, but by HIS Own Blood HE entered in once into the holy place, having obtained eternal redemption for us.

Hebrews 13:12: Wherefore JESUS also, that HE might sanctify the people with HIS Own Blood, suffered without the gate.

Revelation 1:5: And from JESUS CHRIST, WHO is the FAITHFUL WITNESS, and the FIRST BEGOTTEN of the dead, and the PRINCE of the kings of the earth. Unto HIM that loved us, and washed us from our sins in HIS Own Blood,

4. Do Not Despair In These Dark Days

The LORD's Words for Today

(Letter received from our LORD by Susan, May 20, 2012)

"Do not despair in these dark days...."

Now let US begin:

Children, it is I, your LORD:

The hour is approaching for MY Soon Return. So many still do not even know ME. I am a GOD WHO can be known and found. I am a GOD WHO you can come in close to. I am not far away. I am always near to those who seek ME.

Do not despair in these dark days. If you lean on ME, you will be safe. Give ME your all, children. I will take you in MY Loving Arms, hold you close, and keep you safe. I am coming soon to collect MY bride and to put her away to safety. She does not need to fear a thing.

Although the world is getting dark and there are many dark things going on in the world, I will take MY children through the darkest hour. There is nothing that MY bride needs to fear. She is safe under MY Wing. I give her safety even though the earth is turning dark and desolate. I will not forsake her or leave her to face the worst.

She will remain safe until I pull her out to MY Side. Darkness is pouring over the earth. Evil man is growing more evil and his acts against GOD are rising up to MY Throne. I see the acts of evil men all across the land. Nothing gets by ME. All that is hidden to the sight is not hidden from ME. I know all the evil that goes on in the earth. Nothing is not laid bare before MY Throne; I see all…I know all.

Children, the bride is not meant for the dark hour approaching. She is meant for safe keeping. So do not fear what is coming. These are the birth pains. I will put MY bride away to safety.

Are you MY bride?

Encourage each other to seek to be MY bride. She is the one I will bring out of the earth. All others will be lost. Soon I will lift her up into the skies with ME, safe and out of the reach of MY enemy.

Rejoice, for your patience will be rewarded. I am coming with MY Reward. So prepare for MY Return. The hour approaches: stand and look for MY Arrival. Watch for ME! Blessed are those who watch; for those is the Kingdom of heaven.

Precious are they in MY Sight when MY children take flight. I will meet them in the air and wonderful will be their arrival to MY heavenlies. This is MY Gift to MY devoted followers to be freed and live eternally with ME, to share eternal love and laughter with their KING!

Glorious is the way of MY bride. She will be embraced by MY Love for eternity. Come children, come into MY Open, Waiting Arms. This is the hour, children. Grasp MY Truth. Read MY Word. Come to know ME. Lay down your life for ME. Surrender your all to ME. Turn from your evil and follow ME. Repent of your sin. Let ME cover you with MY Blood Covering, MY Blood spilt and the ransom paid for your sin.

I will receive you and call you MY own. So come this day and walk with ME. I will prepare you to live with ME for eternity by the washing of MY Word and the filling of MY SPIRIT.

Come to the BRIDEGROOM. Come let ME Love and hold you for eternity. Leave your troubles and worries behind you. This is salvation…this is freedom…this is yours, I long to give it to you. Come and live with ME in MY Kingdom forever. You are the only one who stands between us. You are the only one who keeps us apart.

The hour is almost up. Where will you be when I come to get MY bride? I cannot take you with ME if you choose against ME.

"Beauty" has not met the great hour that awaits MY bride. She has not yet experienced the ultimate "Beauty" of her GOD. Soon she will understand the meaning of "Beauty."

This IS "LOVE and BEAUTY" Speaking,

Behold your GOD waits on you dear bride…

2 Thessalonians 2:13-17: [13] But we are bound to give thanks always to GOD for you, brethren beloved of the LORD, because GOD hath from the beginning chosen you to salvation through sanctification of the SPIRIT and belief of the truth: [14] Whereunto he called you by our gospel, to the obtaining of the glory of our LORD JESUS CHRIST. [15] Therefore, brethren, stand fast, and hold the traditions which ye have been taught, whether by word, or our epistle. [16] Now our LORD JESUS CHRIST HIMSELF, and GOD, even our FATHER, which hath loved us, and hath given us everlasting consolation and good hope through grace, [17] comfort your hearts, and establish you in every good word and work.

Psalm 36:7: How excellent is thy loving kindness, O GOD! Therefore the children of men put their trust under the shadow of THY Wings.

1 John 1:9: If we confess our sins, HE is faithful and just to forgive us our sins, and to cleanse us from all unrighteousness.

Job 31:4: Doth not HE see my ways, and count all my steps?

Jeremiah 23:24: Can any hide himself in secret places that I shall not see him? Saith the LORD, Do not I fill heaven and earth? Saith the LORD.

Ephesians 5:25-27: [25] Husbands, love your wives, even as CHRIST also loved the church, and gave HIMSELF for it; [26] That HE might sanctify and cleanse it with the washing of water by the Word, [27] That HE might present it to HIMSELF a glorious church, not having spot, or wrinkle, or any such thing; but that it should be holy and without blemish.

2 Chronicles 20:21: And when he had consulted with the people, he appointed singers unto the LORD, and that should praise the beauty of holiness, as they went out before the army, and to say, Praise the LORD; for HIS Mercy endureth for ever.

5. I Take No Pleasure In Punishing Men

Word of the LORD:

"O' the sadness of being apart from GOD..."

(Letter received from our LORD by Susan, May 21, 2012)

Susan, the world is coming apart, daughter. They strive in vain. They seek after the things of the world. I know these people not. They pursue ME not. MY Love is far from them. The world has turned its back to ME.

I grieve over this lost world. It grieves ME daughter. There is much sadness in the world. The world is sad because it is apart from its GOD, the GOD that created it, loves it. This world does not seek ME. What a state of affairs. Soon the world will understand MY Wrath and Rejection. The world will see the meaning of being apart from ME. Soon I will unleash MY Fury and the people will know what it means to be apart from GOD.

I take no pleasure in this world, MY daughter. She goes on without ME. She moves in a direction away from GOD. O' the sadness of being apart from GOD...O' the emptiness and longing of men lost for eternity. I take no pleasure in punishing men. I find no pleasure in sending them away, but they know ME not. They pursue ME not. They choose not to know their GOD. O' if men would seek ME— what happiness I would bestow on them—I would bring down the latter rain—I would fill them with love and happiness.

If men would seek ME out, I would flow MY Love over them and there would be no end in sight of MY Abundant Love. MY Grace and Mercy is endless to those who seek after ME. But for those who reject ME: torrents of sadness and cursing will flow over them.

There is no end to the sadness men face who choose against ME. I am a GOD WHO is not to be mocked!

I remember all the details of the lives of men—those who know ME and those who know ME not. All is laid bare before ME at MY Throne—nothing is hidden. There is no secret from GOD. It is best not to cherish this world, but to be devoted and longing for GOD and MY Ways.

Pursue GOD and find safety. Pursue MY enemy and be lost forever more. The choices are simple, yet men make them complicated as so few turn to ME. So few turn: those who turn, are blessed...those who do not suffer greatly.

Turn today—the hour dwindleth away. These chances will not be here much longer as I am coming to get MY bride and to put her away to safety. I long for MY bride. She is coming with ME soon.

This is LOVE TRIUMPHANT,

The LORD, ALPHA and OMEGA.

Hebrews 3:7-13: [7] Wherefore (as the HOLY GHOST saith, Today if ye will hear his voice, [8] harden not your hearts, as in the provocation, in the day of temptation in the wilderness: [9] When your fathers tempted me, proved me, and saw my works forty years. [10] Wherefore I was grieved with that generation, and said, They do always err in their heart; and they have not known my ways. [11] So I sware in my wrath, They shall not enter into my rest.) [12] Take heed, brethren, lest there be in any of you an evil heart of unbelief, in departing from the Living GOD. [13] But exhort one another daily, while it is called Today; lest any of you be hardened through the deceitfulness of sin.

2 Corinthians 4:4: In whom the god of this world hath blinded the minds of them which believe not, lest the light of the glorious gospel of CHRIST, WHO is the image of GOD, should shine unto them.

Jeremiah 23:24: Can any hide himself in secret places that I shall not see him? saith the LORD. Do not I fill heaven and earth? saith the LORD.

John 3:18-20: [18] He that believeth on HIM is not condemned: but he that believeth not is condemned already, because he hath not believed in the Name of the only begotten SON of GOD. [19] And this is the condemnation, that light is come into the world, and men loved darkness rather than light, because their deeds were evil. [20] For everyone that doeth evil hateth the light, neither cometh to the light, lest his deeds should be reproved.

Proverbs 18:10: The Name of the LORD is a STRONG TOWER: the righteous runneth into it, and is safe.

Revelation 22:13: I am ALPHA and OMEGA, the BEGINNING and the END, the FIRST and the LAST.

The World Is Turning To Evil As Its Master

Word of the LORD:

"The world is turning to evil as its master…"

(Letter received from our FATHER by Susan, May 23, 2012)

Yes daughter, please take down MY Words:

Children, it is I, your FATHER Speaking—I want to address you at this moment:

Soon, very soon, MY SON will be bringing you out of the earth. Yes, this Message is for those who take MY Words seriously, for those who follow hard after ME.

If you are choosing for the world over ME, you will be lost, as I can only have those who pursue ME with an open heart, those who long for ME with sincere desire to follow ME. All others who choose the world and her ways will fall away.

Your GOD, the MOST HIGH, "I AM" desires for all men to be saved. The way to MY Heavenlies is open to whosoever will come and lay down their life and receive the Blood-bought ransom paid by MY SON on Calvary's Cross. This price was paid for you. It is available to you. It is a Gift to you—yours for the asking.

MY Love is so great—I gave MY only SON so that you might have life—eternal life, abundant life, HIS Life for your life. This was the price paid. Now you must decide. Are you willing to lay down your life and receive this free Gift to claim the Prize—eternal glory: dwelling with the Living GOD for all your days?

If you choose against this great Gift, you will experience death, destruction, torment, and be cast away from the Presence of GOD for all eternity. This is the penalty for not receiving this free Gift.

The choice is yours to make. You hold blessings or cursings in your hand—which will you cling to and which will you let go of? I say, cling to blessings: grasp the nail-pierced Hand of MY SON, your LORD and SAVIOR. Denounce the captain of your soul, satan, MY enemy. Step away from his control over your life. Choose this day blessings. Lay your life down at the Feet of MY SON. HE alone is Worthy. HE paid your price and died a humbling death. No mercy was granted HIM by MY enemy and no mercy will be granted to you by him either. He means to steal, kill, and destroy.

The hour is waning, MY children. Precious little time remains. The world is turning to evil as its master. MY Ways have no place in this world anymore. The world does not want to honor ME, GOD anymore. The time is short for this world and its ways. Soon MY children will be removed and the only light remaining will go out.

What choice will you make? Will you lay down your life to follow ME and MY Ways or will you follow hard after MY enemy and his ways? You must choose. I will not wait forever on this evil world whose sin has come up to MY Throne. I cannot tolerate this evil much longer. MY Patience is running out. Although I am LONGSUFFERING, the hour approaches for the capturing away of the bride to her eternal abode and the marriage of MY SON to HIS beloved. It is time for the celebration to begin.

Choose this day blessings. You do not want to be left to face the wrath of MY enemy and what is coming to this earth. Seek ME, Seek MY Face. I am waiting for you to choose. I will not lament over this evil much longer.

I am your FATHER.

Accept the Gift of MY SON WHO died for your sins.

HE is Worthy.

Choose Life.

I await your answer.

Galatians 1:4: WHO gave HIMSELF for our sins, that he might deliver us from this present evil world, according to the Will of GOD and our FATHER:

1 John 2:17: And the world passeth away, and the lust thereof: but he that doeth the Will of GOD abideth for ever.

1 John 3:1: Behold, what manner of love the FATHER hath bestowed upon us, that we should be called the sons of GOD: therefore the world knoweth us not, because it knew HIM not.

2 Corinthians 9:15: Thanks be unto GOD for HIS unspeakable Gift.

Ephesians 2:8: For by grace are ye saved through faith; and that not of yourselves: it is the Gift of GOD:

Deuteronomy 11:26-28: [26] Behold, I set before you this day a blessing and a curse; [27] A blessing, if ye obey the Commandments of the LORD your GOD, which I command you this day: [28] And a curse, if ye will not obey the Commandments of the LORD your GOD, but turn aside out of the way which I command you this day, to go after other gods, which ye have not known.

Philippians 2:8: And being found in fashion as a man, HE humbled HIMSELF, and became obedient unto death, even the death of the cross.

John 3:16: For GOD so loved the world, that HE gave HIS only begotten SON, that whosoever believeth in HIM should not perish, but have everlasting life.

6. It Will Be Just As The Days Of Noah And Lot

The LORD's Words for Today (Posted at www.End-Times-Prophecy.Com)

"It will be just as the days of Noah and Lot..."

(Words given by the LORD to Susan, May 28, 2012)

Daughter, Let us then begin:

These Words are from GOD, the FATHER:

Children, I am your FATHER. I come to you with serious Words. There is a time when MY SON's Blood will not be so easy to access. HIS Name will not roll off the tongue of many—the people will shun HIM. It will not be popular at all to call yourself a "Christian." It will, in fact, be dangerous.

Christians, after MY church is removed, will go underground. Everything I stand for will be rejected by mankind. MY Words will be rejected, MY Truth, MY Righteousness. Even now this spirit is rising, the spirit of antichrist.

You must prepare yourselves children for MY SON's Return to earth, to collect HIS bride. Their betrothal is at the door. Soon this event is about to take place.

Children, prepare to be lifted out to safety as your LORD's Coming is soon. You know it is coming. Those watching will not be caught unawares. Those looking the other way will be left because their hearts are unprepared; they lust for the world, and continue to seek it for answers just as Lot's wife looked back to her demise.

There is nothing but death and destruction when you look to the world. The world only represents the traditions of men and the views formulated by MY enemy. This is the source of the thinking of the world. The world is an enmity to ME. Do not pant after her as if she holds all your answers. She holds only death. Instead, press into your MAKER. Come to ME in humble submission. Lay your life at MY SON's Feet. HE alone holds the key to your salvation. Without HIS Blood Sacrifice on a hard cross, you could not stand before ME in the next life.

Your life of sin will cast you away from ME for all eternity except for the Blood-bought ransom MY SON paid dearly for. Receive it and live, live abundantly in an eternal abode with your GOD, your MAKER, CREATOR. Abundance is yours if you accept freely the gift of your SAVIOR, your KING, MY SON. There is no other way. I will not receive you without HIS Blood Covering. You can only receive this Blood Covering through repentance of a lifetime of sin and through total submission to MY SON as your LORD and MASTER. This is how you will receive access to MY Heavenlies. There is no other way!

Don't be deceived, others will tell you different as deception is running high. There is only ONE PATH, ONE NARROW PATH. It is through MY SON's Gracious Gift that you receive everlasting life in MY Kingdom.

Time is running out for you to make this decision and to prepare your garments through the washing of MY Word. Only through the filling of MY SPIRIT are you ready when MY SON comes for HIS bride.

Children, MY Love is Great, but only a few children will leave with MY SON as only a few are really watching, waiting, and ready.

Read MY Word. This is made clear in MY Word. It will be just as the days of Noah and Lot. So be on guard, vigilant, and watching for this event will come like a thief in the night and many will be caught unawares.

And when I remove MY Great Light from the earth, darkness will pour out like never before. Be ready, as the hour is coming for the bride to come up hither.

FATHER of all

MAKER of all

LORD…MASTER…GOD…CREATOR

Luke 12:53: The father shall be divided against the son, and the son against the father; the mother against the daughter, and the daughter against the mother; the mother in law against her daughter in law, and the daughter in law against her mother in law.

1 John 2:18: Little children, it is the last time: and as ye have heard that antichrist shall come, even now are there many antichrists; whereby we know that it is the last time.

Luke 17:26-32: [26] And as it was in the days of Noah, so shall it be also in the days of the SON of man. [27] They did eat, they drank, they married wives, they were given in marriage, until the day that Noah entered into the ark, and the flood came, and destroyed them all. [28] Likewise also as it was in the days of Lot; they did eat, they drank, they bought, they sold, they planted, they builded; [29] But the same day that Lot went out of Sodom it rained fire and brimstone from heaven, and destroyed them all. [30] Even thus shall it be in the day when the SON of man is revealed. [31] In that day, he which shall be upon the housetop, and his stuff in the house, let him not come down to take it away: and he that is in the field, let him likewise not return back. ³² Remember Lot's wife.

James 4:4: Ye adulterers and adulteresses, know ye not that the friendship of the world is enmity with GOD? Whosoever therefore will be a friend of the world is the enemy of GOD.

John 14:6: JESUS saith unto him, I am the WAY, the TRUTH, and the LIFE: no man cometh unto the FATHER, but by ME.

Matthew 7:14: Because strait is the gate, and narrow is the way, which leadeth unto life, and few there be that find it.

Ephesians 5:25-27: ²⁵ Husbands, love your wives, even as CHRIST also loved the church, and gave HIMSELF for it; ²⁶ That HE might sanctify and cleanse it with the washing of water by the Word, ²⁷ That HE might present it to HIMSELF a glorious church, not having spot, or wrinkle, or any such thing; but that it should be holy and without blemish.

1 Thessalonians 5:2: For yourselves know perfectly that the day of the LORD so cometh as a thief in the night.

7. This Is Your Purpose For Living: To Choose "For" Or "Against" God

Word of the LORD:

"The hour for MY Return to pull MY bride to safety comes and no man can stop it."

(Words given by the LORD to Susan, May 31, 2012)

Yes, MY children, it is I, your LORD:

These Words are true. I am a GOD WHO you can trust. I am a GOD you can believe in. I am everlasting: from Glory to Glory.

MY Kingdom never ends. I am victorious over MY enemies. I shower those who love ME with MY Love. There is no shadow of turning in WHO I am. MY Truth is everlasting. I am the Great "I AM."

MY Word never stops. There is no end in sight of the good I do. Do you want to be part of MY Everlasting Kingdom? You can be. I am a GOD WHO is true to HIS Word. I am an EVERLASTING BEACON of Truth.

You can be with ME for eternity or you can be with MY enemy in everlasting hell. These are your choices. There are but two. Although it would seem there are many options, there are but two choices. Most, sadly, settle for less and hell is their destination. Is this your choice?

This is your purpose for living: to choose "for" or "against" GOD, to determine your final destination—either to MY Kingdom or MY enemy's for all eternity. What direction do you choose to move in? Will you come out with ME to everlasting love, hope, security in this life and the next or will you make your final destination in the deepest pits of hell? If you reject MY Truth, you will send yourself to hell. I cannot lie to you, reject ME and your punishment will be eternal.

How can you avoid this? Submit your life over to ME—your LORD and SAVIOR. MY Name is YEHUSHUA—SAVIOR—MESSIAH. I died in your place to rescue you from your sins, to cover you in MY Blood, to ransom you from death and destruction and the grip of MY enemy. He wants your life too. He means to destroy you and separate us for eternity. You do not need to end your life this way. You can come with ME to MY Eternal Kingdom and share in MY Eternal Inheritance.

All I have is yours if you follow ME. Come to ME; turn your life over to ME fully without regret. Repent of your lifetime of sin and let ME prepare you by giving you new eyes to see MY Truth by filling you completely with MY SPIRIT. HE will come into your life and fill you with HIS SPIRIT, indwelling your spirit; HIS Truth consuming you; renewing your mind to refresh you; make you complete, whole, to take away the devastation of past sins; and to move you to fullness of Life. This is the promise I make for submitting to MY Will: Life everlasting; wholeness of heart; hope eternal; Love supreme. All this is yours for the asking…for the taking.

Submit yourself to MY Will, leave MY enemy's will behind—your self will and be refreshed, relieved of sorrow, pain, and the way of evil that consumes you. This is not MY Way. I come to bring you Life everlasting: so few ever come to know the fullness of MY SPIRIT, to walk fully in MY Truth, MY Will. Too many settle for portions of Truth and give themselves to MY enemy: so few experience the depths of MY Love and walk in the fullness of MY Peace and Calm that passes all understanding.

This is yours even now if you want it. Lay down your life. Give it to ME. Let ME make you into a new person—the person I meant you to be—full of MY SPIRIT and Truth, complete through MY Love, refreshed and walking in MY Will. I created you. MY Will for your life can be yours. Submit your life back to ME and let ME take possession of your soul. What does it all mean if a man gains the whole world but loses HIS soul?

This is the hour of decision, great decision. Who will you go with? Will you go with MY enemy to ultimate destruction or with ME to everlasting peace, love, and life? The choice is yours to make. I can only hold out MY Hand and offer you this choice. Choose this day, who you will serve—a man cannot serve two masters.

Your CREATOR awaits your choice. If you choose against ME, I will depart from you for eternity. Be careful how you choose. Be sober-minded and clear-thinking as your time is limited for making this choice. The hour for MY Return to pull MY bride to safety comes and no man can stop it. Be ready to come with ME when I come for MY bride, MY true church.

Are you ready? Many will be surprised when they find themselves left. There will be much sorrow and weeping for those who choose for the world in these, the final hours. MY Warnings are many: only those who refuse to watch cannot see the signs I am putting forth. Don't be blinded and deceived by the world. She will lead you astray and catch you in a web of deception. Very few are free from this web already. Very few have freed themselves to follow ME fully.

Let ME free you from this world that is falling into chaos and darkness. Your GOD is mighty to save. Come before it is too late. I am giving you Pleadings and Warnings. Come to your senses. Step into MY Light and be saved by MY Truth, MY Word, MY SPIRIT, MY Blood, MY Name. Salvation and Life can be yours. Claim it!

This is your Everlasting LORD.

Eternal GOD.

"I AM"

2 Corinthians 3:18: But we all, with open face beholding as in a glass the glory of the LORD, are changed into the same image from glory to glory, even as by the SPIRIT of the LORD.

James 1:17: Every good gift and every perfect gift is from above, and cometh down from the FATHER of Lights, with WHOM is no variableness, neither shadow of turning.

Psalm 106:48: Blessed be the LORD GOD of Israel from everlasting to everlasting: and let all the people say, Amen. Praise ye the LORD.

Daniel 7:14: And there was given HIM dominion, and glory, and a Kingdom, that all people, nations, and languages, should serve HIM: HIS dominion is an everlasting dominion, which shall not pass away, and HIS Kingdom that which shall not be destroyed.

Mark 3:29: But he that shall blaspheme against the HOLY GHOST hath never forgiveness, but is in danger of eternal damnation.

Colossians 3:24: Knowing that of the LORD ye shall receive the reward of the inheritance: for ye serve the LORD CHRIST.

Revelation 21:7: He that overcometh shall inherit all things; and I will be his GOD, and he shall be MY son.

Matthew 16:26: For what is a man profited, if he shall gain the whole world, and lose his own soul? Or what shall a man give in exchange for his soul?

Joshua 24:15: And if it seem evil unto you to serve the LORD, choose you this day whom ye will serve; whether the gods which your fathers served that were on the other side of the flood, or the gods of the Amorites, in whose land ye dwell: but as for me and my house, we will serve the LORD.

Matthew 6:24: No man can serve two masters: for either he will hate the one, and love the other; or else he will hold to the one, and despise the other. Ye cannot serve GOD and mammon.

John 1:17: For the law was given by Moses, but grace and truth came by JESUS CHRIST.

Ephesians 5:25-26: [25]Husbands, love your wives, even as CHRIST also loved the church, and gave HIMSELF for it; [26] that HE might sanctify and cleanse it with the washing of water by the Word,

Revelation 1:5: And from JESUS CHRIST, WHO is the Faithful WITNESS, and the FIRST BEGOTTEN of the dead, and the PRINCE of the kings of the earth. Unto HIM that loved us, and washed us from our sins in HIS Own Blood,

Luke 11:13: If ye then, being evil, know how to give good gifts unto your children: how much more shall your Heavenly FATHER give the HOLY SPIRIT to them that ask HIM?

Acts 4:12: Neither is there salvation in any other: for there is none other name under heaven given among men, whereby we must be saved.

8. I Want A Pure Bride

The LORD's Words for Today (Posted at www.End-Times-Prophecy.Com)

Word of the LORD:

"I want a pure bride."

(Words Received from Our LORD by Susan, June 4, 2012)

Daughter, you may write MY Words—Let US begin:

Children, it is I, once again, your LORD.

Soon this world will know true wrath. This day is coming, children. The hour approaches. Many do not believe, although many signs have gone out. I have put forth many messages. For these seeking Truth there has been a fountain flowing from MY Throne of Truth and Warnings. Many will be caught off guard, but there will be no excuses for them as MY Word has been available and MY SPIRIT to guide them. It will be a great day of devastation and loss.

Children, Truth flows freely now. Many have access to a bounty of Words from ME about what is coming to the earth and mankind, but few really choose to listen, therefore few will be rescued. This is in MY Word. I have made it clear. This should make you tremble. It should send chills up your spine of a strong desire to follow hard after your LORD and SAVIOR instead of pursuing and playing with the world.

I want a pure bride. This is what I require. Not one whose hands are dirtied by the things of the world. The world is full of filth and distractions from GOD. Only I hold ALL Truth, all other truth or meaning put forth by the world comes straight from the mouth of MY enemy through men who know me not, who pursue ME not. Only by the teachings of MY SPIRIT which is garnered by a complete filling of MY SPIRIT—this is what it takes to be right with GOD, to move toward purity, right-thinking. Only through a filling of MY SPIRIT, a full oil lamp, can you truly pursue holiness and MY Blood-bought Perfection which I endow to mankind received by humble submission and sincere repentance for a lifetime of evil, sin, and rebellion to GOD.

Children the hour is coming for ME to take a prepared bride home to safety. I am only coming for a prepared bride—one who has laid her life before ME, submitted to MY Will, agreed to follow ME above all others. She is fully surrendered. There is no lusting after the world in her heart. Do you see yourself in MY bride? Do you want to be part of this unique group that is MY last remaining light in the world? She alone reflects MY Heart out to a lost world.

Many believe that they are among this group. Many are deceived and do not examine their hearts—so few really want to give ME their all. This is what I ask. This is what I require.

If you pursued ME as the ONE True and Utmost Desire of your heart than I would renew your mind, pour out MY SPIRIT, and bring you to all Truth. This is MY Promise to all who follow MY Commandment to love your LORD GOD with all your heart, soul, mind, and strength.

I will not leave anyone behind who comes after ME with a sincere heart operating out of faith. I cannot go against MY Word. Lay your life before ME in humble repentance. Ask to be filled with MY SPIRIT and to be shown Truth and Salvation and this Gift is yours. I have made it available by the shedding of MY Blood when I stood in for you and paid your ransom for your life of rebellion and sin.

I endured the cross so you can receive the free Gift of Salvation. There is nothing you can do to earn this Salvation, lest you boast. You just need to present your life to ME. Then, I will take your life and prepare you to come with ME away to MY heavenlies for safekeeping, away from a world that rejects its GOD.

Join ME today. Join in the joy that is coming for those who leave the will of MY enemy and walk into MY Truth. Pleasant is the life of those who are right with their GOD. Blessings, peace, love await those who live in humble submission to GOD.

Childlike faith is what I require. Make this transaction today. Exchange the old man for the new man. Come and be renewed; experience refreshment through MY Blood and MY SPIRIT.

I, your LORD and the bride say, "Come!"

Matthew 24:33-34: [33]So likewise ye, when ye shall see all these things, know that it is near, even at the doors. [34]Verily I say unto you, This generation shall not pass, till all these things be fulfilled.

Luke 17:26-30: [26]And as it was in the days of Noah, so shall it be also in the days of the SON of man. [27] They did eat, they drank, they married wives, they were given in marriage, until the day that Noah entered into the ark, and the flood came, and destroyed them all. [28]Likewise also as it was in the days of Lot; they did eat, they drank, they bought, they sold, they planted, they builded; [29]But the same day that Lot went out of Sodom it rained fire and brimstone from heaven, and destroyed them all. [30]Even thus shall it be in the day when the SON of man is revealed.

1 Corinthians 2:10-13: [10]But GOD hath revealed them unto us by HIS SPIRIT: for the SPIRIT searcheth all things, yea, the deep things of GOD. [11]For what man knoweth the things of a man, save the spirit of man which is in him? Even so the things of GOD knoweth no man, but the SPIRIT of GOD. [12]Now we have received, not the spirit of the world, but the SPIRIT which is of GOD; that we might know the things that are freely given to us of GOD. [13]Which things also we speak, not in the words which man's wisdom teacheth, but which the HOLY GHOST teacheth; comparing spiritual things with spiritual.

Matthew 25:4: But the wise took oil in their vessels with their lamps.

Mark 12:30: And thou shalt love the LORD thy GOD with all thy heart, and with all thy soul, and with all thy mind, and with all thy strength: this is the first commandment.

Ephesians 2:7-9: [7]That in the ages to come HE might shew the exceeding riches of HIS grace in HIS kindness toward us through CHRIST JESUS. [8]For by grace are ye saved through faith; and that not of yourselves: it is the gift of GOD: [9]Not of works, lest any man should boast.

Mark 10:15: Verily I say unto you, Whosoever shall not receive the Kingdom of GOD as a little child, he shall not enter therein.

Colossians 3:9-10: [9]Lie not one to another, seeing that ye have put off the old man with his deeds; [10] And have put on the new man, which is renewed in knowledge after the image of HIM that created him:

9. Come Away From The Path Of Destruction You Are On

"Don't waste another day moving on the broad road to destruction."

(Words Received from Our LORD by Susan, June 5, 2012)

Let US begin:

Children, it is I, your LORD—Great and Mighty Everlasting KING.

Soon, I am coming to receive the bride unto MYSELF. She is about to be removed from the earth. To many this will be a great surprise. To MY bride it will be an expected delight because MY bride is watching…waiting…anticipating…MY Return.

Children, I am coming for a bride who is anxiously looking forward to MY Return. She is small in numbers. Most do not want to hear of MY Soon Coming. This does not fit with their plans. It does not work into their future planning's.

Children, it is I, WHO plans the future. I know the beginning from the end. You can either fall into MY Planning, MY Will for your life by surrendering your life over to ME completely or all your planning apart from MY Will is devised for you by MY enemy.

Do you see this MY children? What you believe to be your own future plans are actually only the carefully laid plans of MY enemy. All his plans for you are for your ultimate destruction and separation from your GOD CREATOR for eternity.

I have plans for you too, MY children, to give you a hope and a future, but MY children you must come into MY Will, MY Perfect Will to realize these plans I have set before you. You must come to ME in humble surrender and serious repentance for your past life of sin so that you can henceforth move into MY Perfect Will for your life.

Once you have chosen to make ME your LORD and MASTER, I will take you by the hand and set you on the straight path, the narrow road toward MY Eternal Kingdom. Your life will then have true meaning and you will receive peace, and righteousness, and understanding for the things of GOD. MY SPIRIT will guide you and lead you into everlasting ways. This is the path your life was meant to take.

Come away from the path of destruction you are on. The way of the world looks so right, but the way of the world is a way of destruction leading to everlasting hell and torment. This is not the direction I planned for you to move in. Your life can take on so much more meaning and you can have the wholeness that you were meant to dwell in by the power and filling of MY SPIRIT.

Come to ME. Let ME show you the way. Walk the way that I had prepared for you in advance—the way everlasting. There is no other way to go to receive life everlasting.

Today you can make this change. You can leave the path of destruction and join ME on the right road to MY Everlasting Kingdom with the true plan I, GOD, have prepared for your life, the life I Created.

This choice is yours. No one can make it for you. You must choose. Will you come with ME or will you go by the way of destruction with MY enemy? There are only two roads by which you can go.

The hour is short. Make your way quickly to the right path. Don't waste another day moving on the broad road to destruction. MY

Hand is stretched out to take you with ME when I come for MY bride.

I am GOD, Great to Deliver, but I will not wait forever on MY children. There are already so many who have made wrong choices lost on the broad road to destruction. The hour is upon this evil earth and evil man who have chosen against ME. Soon the bride will be removed to safety. Are you coming?

I am THE GOD, WHO is AWESOME to SAVE!

JEHOVAH JIRAH.

2 Timothy 4:8: Henceforth there is laid up for me a crown of righteousness, which the LORD, the Righteous JUDGE, shall give me at that day: and not to me only, but unto all them also that love HIS appearing.

Isaiah 46:9-10: [9]Remember the former things of old: for I am GOD, and there is none else; I am GOD, and there is none like ME,[10]Declaring the end from the beginning, and from ancient times the things that are not yet done, saying, MY counsel shall stand, and I will do all MY pleasure:

2 Corinthians 4:4: In whom the god of this world hath blinded the minds of them which believe not, lest the light of the glorious gospel of CHRIST, WHO is the IMAGE of GOD, should shine unto them.

Ephesians 2:2: Wherein in time past ye walked according to the course of this world, according to the prince of the power of the air, the spirit that now worketh in the children of disobedience:

Romans 12:2: And be not conformed to this world: but be ye transformed by the renewing of your mind, that ye may prove what is that good, and acceptable, and perfect, Will of GOD.

Jeremiah 29:11: For I know the thoughts that I think toward you, saith the LORD, thoughts of peace, and not of evil, to give you an expected end.

My True Followers Recognize The Hour They Are Living In

LORD's Words for Today (Posted at www.End-Times-Prophecy.Com)

Word of the LORD:

"You, MY children, are dying from lack of knowledge."

(Words Received from Our LORD by Susan, June 12, 2012)

Yes daughter, listen to MY Words:

Children, it is I, your LORD Speaking. The hour comes for MY Return. Children, are you ready?

Are you watching for ME? Do you know this is what I require of you? Isn't this in MY Book? Have you not read this in MY Word? Then why do so few of you comply to MY Request? Why do I find so few willing to watch for ME, look for ME, pursue ME, follow ME? MY Word is very clear.

If you are not looking for ME, you are distracted by something other than GOD. Something else is taking your time, your attention, your focus, and it is not ME, because MY true followers recognize the hour they are living in and the time. They are watching for ME and focused on ME. So if you are not seeking ME and focused elsewhere, you are in a dangerous position and MY enemy has you firmly in his grip.

You, MY children, are dying from lack of knowledge. You cannot be washed by MY Word if you are not in MY Word! You cannot receive MY Word through the teachings of MY SPIRIT if you do not possess MY SPIRIT. If you do not have HIM in all HIS Fullness you are therefore lukewarm and in a dangerous condition with your GOD.

Do you not understand that I hold life in MY Hand? I brought you into the world and I will take you out of this world. It is up to you what direction you leave to, when you leave. Will you come out with ME as MY bride to a beautiful home in the heavenlies or will you be cast away into hell apart from ME for eternity? Do not count on being left behind, as many will be caught in sudden destruction following the removal of the church. Don't play games with your eternal soul.

This is serious MY children. You believe you have all the time in the world to relax and enjoy life and the things of the world, but there is a great wave of darkness moving over the land and if you don't move quickly into MY Light, you will be caught in the darkness and there will be no turning back. I cannot rescue you once the enemy has you in his clutches. So many have fallen away as the road is broad to destruction—eternal destruction. This is most serious. You are playing with fire if you think otherwise.

Do not turn away from ME to other lesser gods and towards the distractions of the world and MY enemy. He does not care how you are deceived. He only wants your destruction—he does not care how you arrive to it.

You can be saved from this heartache MY children, as I have planned for your rescue if you would only turn from your wicked ways and follow ME, your SAVIOR. I have the answers. You cannot find them anywhere else. Don't be deceived—there is much deception and it is coming from all sides around you. You can only trust MY Word and ME.

I ask you to give ME your life in a full surrender. Repent of your sins with a humble heart. Then I can come and reside within you, make you complete, fill you completely. WE will reside within you. Your life can then know wholeness, peace, and your soul will be satisfied because you are right with your GOD, walking in MY Will for your life. Do not settle for anything less. Anything less will lead you to destruction.

I only speak these Words out of a Heart of Love and Truth. I desire for you to be saved and kept from the great evil that is even now coming to the earth. Allow ME to save you, fill you with MY SPIRIT, cover you with MY Blood, set you free from sin's bondage, and the control of MY enemy who reigns over you. If you are not of ME— you are being used by MY enemy for purposes of his destruction against MY Kingdom and you will be accountable for the part you play in destruction in this life: lost souls, lost rewards in MY Eternal Kingdom. There are things you cannot readily see, but your unwillingness to surrender fully to ME puts you outside of MY Will and makes you an agent of evil against MY Kingdom and one of MY rebellious children.

Lay down your weapons of destruction: your rebellion, your lawlessness, acts of sedition, and turn to ME to receive MY Blood and to walk in holiness and HOLY SPIRIT Fire! This is your heritage to claim, but you must desire to leave your worldly lust and to come into MY Open, Saving Arms!

I am waiting children, to save you,

Turn and come home!

Mark 13:28-31: ²⁸Now learn a parable of the fig tree; When her branch is yet tender, and putteth forth leaves, ye know that summer is near: ²⁹So ye in like manner, when ye shall see these things come to pass, know that it is nigh, even at the doors. ³⁰Verily I say unto you, that this generation shall not pass, till all these things be done. ³¹Heaven and earth shall pass away: but my words shall not pass away.

Mark 13:34-37: ³⁴For the SON of man is as a man taking a far journey, who left his house, and gave authority to his servants, and to every man his work, and commanded the porter to watch. ³⁵Watch ye therefore: for ye know not when the master of the house cometh, at even, or at midnight, or at the cockcrowing, or in the morning: ³⁶Lest coming suddenly he find you sleeping. ³⁷And what I say unto you I say unto all, Watch.

Hosea 4:6: MY people are destroyed for lack of knowledge: because thou hast rejected knowledge, I will also reject thee, that thou shalt be no priest to ME: seeing thou hast forgotten the law of thy GOD, I will also forget thy children.

Matthew 7:13: Enter ye in at the strait gate: for wide is the gate, and broad is the way, that leadeth to destruction, and many there be which go in thereat:

Isaiah 30:1-3: Woe to the rebellious children, saith the LORD, that take counsel, but not of ME; and that cover with a covering, but not of MY SPIRIT, that they may add sin to sin: ²That walk to go down into Egypt, and have not asked at MY Mouth; to strengthen themselves in the strength of Pharaoh, and to trust in the shadow of Egypt! ³Therefore shall the strength of Pharaoh be your shame, and the trust in the shadow of Egypt your confusion.

1 Corinthians 2:11: For what man knoweth the things of a man, save the spirit of man which is in him? Even so the things of GOD knoweth no man, but the SPIRIT of GOD.

Job 9:12: Behold, HE taketh away, who can hinder HIM? Who will say unto HIM, What doest THOU?

1 Thessalonians 5:3: For when they shall say, Peace and safety; then sudden destruction cometh upon them, as travail upon a woman with child; and they shall not escape.

Psalms 118:8: It is better to trust in the LORD than to put confidence in man.

Isaiah 58:11: And the LORD shall guide thee continually, and satisfy thy soul in drought, and make fat thy bones: and thou shalt be like a watered garden, and like a spring of water, whose waters fail not.

Nehemiah 9:17-20: ¹⁷And refused to obey, neither were mindful of THY wonders that THOU didst among them; but hardened their necks, and in their rebellion appointed a captain to return to their bondage: but THOU art a GOD ready to pardon, gracious and merciful, slow to anger, and of great kindness, and forsookest them not. ¹⁸Yea, when they had made them a molten calf, and said, This is thy God that brought thee up out of Egypt, and had wrought great provocations; ¹⁹Yet thou in THY Manifold Mercies forsookest them not in the wilderness: the pillar of the cloud departed not from them by day, to lead them in the way; neither the pillar of fire by night, to shew them light, and the way wherein they should go. ²⁰THOU gavest also THY Good SPIRIT to instruct them, and withheldest not THY manna from their mouth, and gavest them water for their thirst.

The Timing Is Now For My Return !

"Children, MY Word does not falter."

(Words Received from Our LORD by Susan, June 13, 2012)

Daughter, it is your LORD Speaking. I am ready to give you a new letter, so let US begin:

Children it is I, your LORD. I recognize that very few are paying attention to the hour they are living in—very few really want to believe that MY Coming is so soon. But the Truth is, it is right around the corner…

Few want to believe. There are only a few who want to leave this world behind and who want to come with ME to everlasting peace and tranquility to the eternal homes I have prepared. The world is just too enticing.

If you read and studied MY Word, you would see that MY Signs, Warnings, and messengers I send out are very clearly showing you what was told so long ago would happen. Children, MY Word does not falter. I am not a man that I should lie. When you begin to see all these things come to pass, then you know I am standing right at the door and MY Coming is near.

I have made this all very clear. All these events that I said would happen at this hour will not come together again at a future date— the timing is now for MY Return!

You do not see the nearness of MY Coming because you refuse to look! The prophecies that I set out before you are coming to pass, just as they were told about so very long ago. Why do you doubt MY Book so? Why do you mistrust ME so? Why are you so certain that the world has all your answers? Why are you so doubtful? Could it be because you lack faith in MY Word and would rather follow MY enemy? He is more than happy to have you following him. He will lead you to your demise!

Children, listen as I bring you this Truth: MY enemy wants to destroy you. He wants to carry you away to destruction. This is his great desire. He is bent on revenge. Don't believe him, as he is the father of lies. Too many have fallen into his web of deception, too many will never know MY Heavenlies. Don't be so sure of yourself—MY opponent is cunning and you are no match for him apart from ME: your GUIDE, your SAVIOR, your KING. Only by MY Power, Might, and Name can this opponent be conquered. So come and lay your life down before ME and admit you need a SAVIOR and I will set you free from the bondage of sin and the treachery of evil.

The world is growing black with sin, darkness, evil, and soon MY Light will be completely snuffed out after MY bride comes up to her safe home with ME, her KING EVERLASTING. Open your eyes to Truth. Read MY Word, get to know ME, your SAVIOR. I can be trusted. You have only moments to go before I remove MY chosen people. Surrender your life to ME. I want to take you with ME.

MY Cup runneth over for you.

Drink freely of the LIVING WATERS. Come drink!

Proverbs 30:5: Every word of GOD is pure: HE is a SHIELD unto them that put their trust in HIM.

Numbers 23:19: GOD is not a man, that HE should lie; neither the SON of man, that HE should repent: hath HE said, and shall HE not do it? Or hath HE spoken, and shall HE not make it good?

Matthew 24:33-34: [33]So likewise ye, when ye shall see all these things, know that it is near, even at the doors. [34]Verily I say unto you, This generation shall not pass, till all these things be fulfilled.

John 10:10: The thief cometh not, but for to steal, and to kill, and to destroy: I am come that they might have life, and that they might have it more abundantly.

John 8:44: Ye are of your father the devil, and the lusts of your father ye will do. He was a murderer from the beginning, and abode not in the truth, because there is no truth in him. When he speaketh a lie, he speaketh of his own: for he is a liar, and the father of it.

Psalms 48:14: For this GOD is our GOD forever and ever: HE will be our GUIDE even unto death.

Romans 13:1: Let every soul be subject unto the higher powers. For there is no power but of GOD: the powers that be are ordained of GOD.

Revelation 17:14: These shall make war with the LAMB, and the LAMB shall overcome them: for HE is LORD of lords, and KING of kings: and they that are with HIM are called, and chosen, and faithful.

Psalms 116:13: I will take the cup of salvation, and call upon the Name of the LORD.

Psalms 23:5: THOU preparest a table before me in the presence of mine enemies: THOU anointest my head with oil; my cup runneth over.

Song of Solomon 4:15: A fountain of gardens, a well of living waters, and streams from Lebanon.

Jeremiah 17:13: O LORD, the HOPE of Israel, all that forsake THEE shall be ashamed, and they that depart from me shall be written in the earth, because they have forsaken the LORD, the FOUNTAIN of LIVING WATERS.

You Believe You Have All The Time In The World…

The LORD's Words: "Children, MY Word does not falter."

The LORD's Words for Today (Posted at www.End-Times-Prophecy.Com)

Word of the LORD:

"You, MY children, are dying from lack of knowledge."

(Words Received from Our LORD by Susan, June 12, 2012)

Yes daughter, listen to MY Words:

Children, it is I, your LORD Speaking. The hour comes for MY Return. Children, are you ready?

Are you watching for ME? Do you know this is what I require of you? Isn't this in MY Book? Have you not read this in MY Word? Then why do so few of you comply to MY Request? Why do I find so few willing to watch for ME, look for ME, pursue ME, follow ME? MY Word is very clear.

If you are not looking for ME, you are distracted by something other than GOD. Something else is taking your time, your attention, your focus, and it is not ME, because MY true followers recognize the hour they are living in and the time. They are watching for ME and focused on ME. So if you are not seeking ME and focused elsewhere, you are in a dangerous position and MY enemy has you firmly in his grip.

You, MY children, are dying from lack of knowledge. You cannot be washed by MY Word if you are not in MY Word! You cannot receive MY Word through the teachings of MY SPIRIT if you do not possess MY SPIRIT. If you do not have HIM in all HIS Fullness you are therefore lukewarm and in a dangerous condition with your GOD.

Do you not understand that I hold life in MY Hand? I brought you into the world and I will take you out of this world. It is up to you what direction you leave to, when you leave. Will you come out with ME as MY bride to a beautiful home in the heavenlies or will you be cast away into hell apart from ME for eternity? Do not count on being left behind, as many will be caught in sudden destruction following the removal of the church. Don't play games with your eternal soul.

This is serious MY children. You believe you have all the time in the world to relax and enjoy life and the things of the world, but there is a great wave of darkness moving over the land and if you don't move quickly into MY Light, you will be caught in the darkness and there will be no turning back. I cannot rescue you once the enemy has you in his clutches. So many have fallen away as the road is broad to destruction—eternal destruction. This is most serious. You are playing with fire if you think otherwise.

Do not turn away from ME to other lesser gods and towards the distractions of the world and MY enemy. He does not care how you are deceived. He only wants your destruction—he does not care how you arrive to it.

You can be saved from this heartache MY children, as I have planned for your rescue if you would only turn from your wicked ways and follow ME, your SAVIOR. I have the answers. You cannot find them anywhere else. Don't be deceived—there is much deception and it is coming from all sides around you. You can only trust MY Word and ME.

I ask you to give ME your life in a full surrender. Repent of your sins with a humble heart. Then I can come and reside within you, make you complete, fill you completely. WE will reside within you. Your life can then know wholeness, peace, and your soul will be satisfied because you are right with your GOD, walking in MY Will for your life. Do not settle for anything less. Anything less will lead you to destruction.

I only speak these Words out of a Heart of Love and Truth. I desire for you to be saved and kept from the great evil that is even now coming to the earth. Allow ME to save you, fill you with MY SPIRIT, cover you with MY Blood, set you free from sin's bondage, and the control of MY enemy who reigns over you. If you are not of ME—you are being used by MY enemy for purposes of his destruction against MY Kingdom and you will be accountable for the part you play in destruction in this life: lost souls, lost rewards in MY Eternal Kingdom. There are things you cannot readily see, but your unwillingness to surrender fully to ME puts you outside of MY Will and makes you an agent of evil against MY Kingdom and one of MY rebellious children.

Lay down your weapons of destruction: your rebellion, your lawlessness, acts of sedition, and turn to ME to receive MY Blood and to walk in holiness and HOLY SPIRIT Fire! This is your heritage to claim, but you must desire to leave your worldly lust and to come into MY Open, Saving Arms!

I am waiting children, to save you,

Turn and come home!

Mark 13:28-31: ²⁸Now learn a parable of the fig tree; When her branch is yet tender, and putteth forth leaves, ye know that summer is near: ²⁹So ye in like manner, when ye shall see these things come to pass, know that it is nigh, even at the doors. ³⁰Verily I say unto you, that this generation shall not pass, till all these things be done. ³¹Heaven and earth shall pass away: but my words shall not pass away.

Mark 13:34-37: ³⁴For the SON of man is as a man taking a far journey, who left his house, and gave authority to his servants, and to every man his work, and commanded the porter to watch. ³⁵Watch ye therefore: for ye know not when the master of the house cometh, at even, or at midnight, or at the cockcrowing, or in the morning: ³⁶Lest coming suddenly he find you sleeping. ³⁷And what I say unto you I say unto all, Watch.

Hosea 4:6: MY people are destroyed for lack of knowledge: because thou hast rejected knowledge, I will also reject thee, that thou shalt be no priest to ME: seeing thou hast forgotten the law of thy GOD, I will also forget thy children.

Matthew 7:13: Enter ye in at the strait gate: for wide is the gate, and broad is the way, that leadeth to destruction, and many there be which go in thereat:

Isaiah 30:1-3: Woe to the rebellious children, saith the LORD, that take counsel, but not of ME; and that cover with a covering, but not of MY SPIRIT, that they may add sin to sin: [2]That walk to go down into Egypt, and have not asked at MY Mouth; to strengthen themselves in the strength of Pharaoh, and to trust in the shadow of Egypt! [3]Therefore shall the strength of Pharaoh be your shame, and the trust in the shadow of Egypt your confusion.

1 Corinthians 2:11: For what man knoweth the things of a man, save the spirit of man which is in him? Even so the things of GOD knoweth no man, but the SPIRIT of GOD.

Job 9:12: Behold, HE taketh away, who can hinder HIM? Who will say unto HIM, What doest THOU?

1 Thessalonians 5:3: For when they shall say, Peace and safety; then sudden destruction cometh upon them, as travail upon a woman with child; and they shall not escape.

Psalms 118:8: It is better to trust in the LORD than to put confidence in man.

Isaiah 58:11: And the LORD shall guide thee continually, and satisfy thy soul in drought, and make fat thy bones: and thou shalt be like a watered garden, and like a spring of water, whose waters fail not.

Nehemiah 9:17-20: [17]And refused to obey, neither were mindful of THY wonders that THOU didst among them; but hardened their necks, and in their rebellion appointed a captain to return to their bondage: but THOU art a GOD ready to pardon, gracious and merciful, slow to anger, and of great kindness, and forsookest them not. ¹⁸Yea, when they had made them a molten calf, and said, This is thy God that brought thee up out of Egypt, and had wrought great provocations; ¹⁹Yet thou in THY Manifold Mercies forsookest them not in the wilderness: the pillar of the cloud departed not from them by day, to lead them in the way; neither the pillar of fire by night, to shew them light, and the way wherein they should go. ²⁰THOU gavest also THY Good SPIRIT to instruct them, and withheldest not THY manna from their mouth, and gavest them water for their thirst.

Few Want To Believe

"Children, MY Word does not falter."

(Words Received from Our LORD by Susan, June 13, 2012)

Daughter, it is your LORD Speaking. I am ready to give you a new letter, so let US begin:

Children it is I, your LORD. I recognize that very few are paying attention to the hour they are living in—very few really want to believe that MY Coming is so soon. But the Truth is, it is right around the corner...

Few want to believe. There are only a few who want to leave this world behind and who want to come with ME to everlasting peace and tranquility to the eternal homes I have prepared. The world is just too enticing.

If you read and studied MY Word, you would see that MY Signs, Warnings, and messengers I send out are very clearly showing you what was told so long ago would happen. Children, MY Word does not falter. I am not a man that I should lie. When you begin to see all these things come to pass, then you know I am standing right at the door and MY Coming is near.

I have made this all very clear. All these events that I said would happen at this hour will not come together again at a future date—the timing is now for MY Return!

You do not see the nearness of MY Coming because you refuse to look! The prophecies that I set out before you are coming to pass, just as they were told about so very long ago. Why do you doubt MY Book so? Why do you mistrust ME so? Why are you so certain that the world has all your answers? Why are you so doubtful? Could it be because you lack faith in MY Word and would rather follow MY enemy? He is more than happy to have you following him. He will lead you to your demise!

Children, listen as I bring you this Truth: MY enemy wants to destroy you. He wants to carry you away to destruction. This is his great desire. He is bent on revenge. Don't believe him, as he is the father of lies. Too many have fallen into his web of deception, too many will never know MY Heavenlies. Don't be so sure of yourself—MY opponent is cunning and you are no match for him apart from ME: your GUIDE, your SAVIOR, your KING. Only by MY Power, Might, and Name can this opponent be conquered. So come and lay your life down before ME and admit you need a SAVIOR and I will set you free from the bondage of sin and the treachery of evil.

The world is growing black with sin, darkness, evil, and soon MY Light will be completely snuffed out after MY bride comes up to her safe home with ME, her KING EVERLASTING. Open your eyes to Truth. Read MY Word, get to know ME, your SAVIOR. I can be trusted. You have only moments to go before I remove MY chosen people. Surrender your life to ME. I want to take you with ME.

MY Cup runneth over for you.

Drink freely of the LIVING WATERS. Come drink!

Proverbs 30:5: Every word of GOD is pure: HE is a SHIELD unto them that put their trust in HIM.

Numbers 23:19: GOD is not a man, that HE should lie; neither the SON of man, that HE should repent: hath HE said, and shall HE not do it? Or hath HE spoken, and shall HE not make it good?

Matthew 24:33-34: [33]So likewise ye, when ye shall see all these things, know that it is near, even at the doors. [34]Verily I say unto you, This generation shall not pass, till all these things be fulfilled.

John 10:10: The thief cometh not, but for to steal, and to kill, and to destroy: I am come that they might have life, and that they might have it more abundantly.

John 8:44: Ye are of your father the devil, and the lusts of your father ye will do. He was a murderer from the beginning, and abode not in the truth, because there is no truth in him. When he speaketh a lie, he speaketh of his own: for he is a liar, and the father of it.

Psalms 48:14: For this GOD is our GOD forever and ever: HE will be our GUIDE even unto death.

Romans 13:1: Let every soul be subject unto the higher powers. For there is no power but of GOD: the powers that be are ordained of GOD.

Revelation 17:14: These shall make war with the LAMB, and the LAMB shall overcome them: for HE is LORD of lords, and KING of kings: and they that are with HIM are called, and chosen, and faithful.

Psalms 116:13: I will take the cup of salvation, and call upon the Name of the LORD.

Psalms 23:5: THOU preparest a table before me in the presence of mine enemies: THOU anointest my head with oil; my cup runneth over.

Song of Solomon 4:15: A fountain of gardens, a well of living waters, and streams from Lebanon.

Jeremiah 17:13: O LORD, the HOPE of Israel, all that forsake THEE shall be ashamed, and they that depart from me shall be written in the earth, because they have forsaken the LORD, the FOUNTAIN of LIVING WATERS.

10. So Few Are Listening

The LORD's Words: "So few are listening...so few are paying attention."

Words of the LORD:

"So few are listening...so few are paying attention."

(Words Received from Our LORD by Susan, June 20, 2012)

MY daughter I am ready to give you Words. Listen carefully as I give you Words:

Children, the hour approaches for MY Return: so few are listening...so few are paying attention. MY Words are falling on death ears, ears that are closed. I am crying out to whoever will come to ME. MY desire is that all men would be saved from the wrath that lies ahead for all mankind.

An evil day is coming. It is soon to arrive. MY people think this is a fable. O' they read MY Words, but it does not sink in. I outlined what to look for and all I said would happen is happening, yet MY people believe ME not and they run after the world. I am not acknowledged. MY Words fall over the people and they do not see them going by. They disregard them and they do not change their ways. They refuse to wash in the water of MY Words and purge their spirit with the brightness of MY SPIRIT. Without MY SPIRIT in all HIS Fullness presiding over your spirit how can you be cleaned and ready when I come for MY children? I am only coming for those with full lamps. Doesn't MY Word speak of this?

Where are your lamps MY children? Are they full or half empty? It is essential to have a full lamp. Without all of MY Oil you cannot be purged and cleaned for MY Presence. I require a clean and chaste bride to stand before ME and to join ME at MY Wedding Table.

MY SPIRIT can only indwell you if you give HIM permission to come in. For this I need a full surrender, humble submission to MY Will. Without this surrender, MY SPIRIT will not intrude on your space. HE will not force HIS entry into your life. This exchange is all done by permission. You must give MY SPIRIT access. You must choose. You have free will.

I am a Humble GOD. I do not make unreasonable demands. I only call and invite you to partake and sup with ME to join ME for eternity, to live with ME in MY Kingdom, MY Eternal Kingdom. You, however, have a choice and you may choose to live outside MY Kingdom.

This choice to be apart from ME will cast you from MY Presence to hell. I am a GOD of truthfulness.

Choose against ME and you will live in outer darkness. The lake of fire will be your destination, a place of torment and torture for eternity. This is MY Word—MY Word changes not.

So the hour draws near for MY Return. Let these Words bring you to the end of yourself and to a full surrender to ME. I desire to give you MY All, to bring you into abundant living—fullness of Heart, overflowing peace and tranquility, right standing with GOD.

All this can be yours for the asking. I give freely. You cannot earn it or work for it. No task can secure it for you. Only MY Bloodshed on a humbling cross can purchase your soul and bring you salvation and everlasting life in MY Heavenlies.

Be aware that the hour is closing in for MY Return to retrieve MY bride. Will you be among MY bride—this unique group of MY followers, GOD's chosen?

The invitation is extended. Don't reject MY Offer. Soon this offer will be withdrawn. The door will close and MY Hand will pull away as I Return with MY bride to OUR Home in the Heavens and OUR Wedding Celebration.

Children, you must choose.

I place life before you.

This is your Enduring KING.

Come, the Banquet Awaits!

1 Timothy 2:3-6: ³For this is good and acceptable in the sight of GOD our SAVIOUR;⁴WHO will have all men to be saved, and to come unto the knowledge of the truth. ⁵For there is One GOD, and One MEDIATOR between GOD and men, the man CHRIST JESUS; ⁶WHO gave HIMSELF a ransom for all, to be testified in due time.

Ephesians5:26-27: ²⁶That he might sanctify and cleanse it with the washing of water by the Word, ²⁷That HE might present it to HIMSELF a glorious church, not having spot, or wrinkle, or any such thing; but that it should be Holy and without blemish.

Matthew 25—Parable of the 10 virgins

Philippians 2:8: And being found in fashion as a man, HE humbled HIMSELF, and became obedient unto death, even the death of the cross.

Revelation 19:9: And he saith unto me, Write, Blessed are they which are called unto the Marriage Supper of the LAMB. And he saith unto me, These are the true sayings of GOD.

Luke 12:5: But I will forewarn you whom ye shall fear: Fear HIM, which after HE hath killed hath power to cast into hell; yea, I say unto you, Fear HIM.

Psalm 31:5: Into THINE Hand I commit my spirit: THOU hast redeemed me, O LORD GOD of Truth.

Revelation 20:15: And whosoever was not found written in the Book of Life was cast into the lake of fire.

Revelation 14:11: And the smoke of their torment ascendeth up for ever and ever: and they have no rest day nor night, who worship the beast and his image, and whosoever receiveth the mark of his name.

Isaiah 40:8: The grass withereth, the flower fadeth: but the Word of our GOD shall stand for ever.

Matthew 25:10: And while they went to buy, the bridegroom came; and they that were ready went in with him to the marriage: and the door was shut.

Psalm 93:2: THY Throne is established of old: THOU art from everlasting.

11. I Cannot Take You If You ... Ignore MY Instructions

Words of the LORD:

Repent! Repent! Repent!

(Words Received from Our LORD by Susan, June 22, 2012)

Listen to MY Words. Here is what I have to say:

Children, you believe there is much time ahead, but the hour is waning for everyone. Listen carefully, MY children. I want to give you instructions. MY Coming is at hand. The time you are being given now is grace. MY Grace is great, but soon limited as I will shut off MY Hand of Grace to those left behind after I remove MY bride from the earth.

She is coming out with ME because I desire her presence and I plan to keep her safe. She is made ready. Her beauty is eternal. I have made her ready. I have given her MY Beauty. MY Love for her is eternal: I long to be near her and to bring her to her eternal home.

You must make yourself ready. I cannot take you if you choose to ignore MY Instructions. I am clear in MY Word. Prepare, for the hour is at hand. Wash in MY Blood. Come clean in MY Blood.

Children: REPENT! REPENT! REPENT!

This is vital instruction. All must repent to enter MY Pearly Gates! All MUST wash in MY Blood! Forgive those around you. Surrender to ME: lay your life at MY Feet. Make no reservations when you come—reserve nothing to yourself.

Turn in your entire life. Give it over to ME. Let ME have it and I will fill it. MY Fullness will consume you and there will be no more room for evil. I must have your attention though, your full attention. If you leave the enemy any part of yourself in submission to ME then he will take it and corrupt it, pervert it, control it, and your life will be compromised and your compromise will be your undoing.

MY enemy is looking for a toehold. He just wants a little space in your life to move in. Destruction is his intent, your destruction. Be very careful and wary. This is the hour of great deception. Don't be deceived. Come in close to ME. There is no other way. Only by MY Light are you saved.

I want to reveal MY Heart to you: share deep intimacies with you. This is not a request—it is a requirement to MY Kingdom—MY Salvation. Don't be fooled. Many believe differently and deceive themselves greatly.

Many believe they can engage themselves with the world and the things thereof and also engage with ME. What deception and misleading. I will not be shared with another—I am a Jealous LOVER. I am a Jealous HUSBAND. Do not believe you can love the world and ME Both when you come before ME. And the things of the world you hold tightly in your hand will not save you. None of it will mean anything. It will burn up and you will be cast away from ME for eternity.

Take these Words to heart. They are solid. Review MY Word and see this Truth for yourself. Don't play with your destiny, like so many do. Regrets are eternal for those who gambled with their lives. Play with the devil and your play time will turn to eternal hell.

I bring you Truth now. Soon, this Truth will be hard to find. MY Words are unchanging. Grasp Truth. Read MY Word. I am the Sure ROUTE. Take MY Hand. Soon, I will deliver MY bride and your chance will be over.

MY Patience is running out. Don't delay making your decision. MY children, come into MY Waiting Arms.

I am your LORD Eternal.

Everlasting to Everlasting.

Psalm 90:17: And let the beauty of the LORD our GOD be upon us: and establish THOU the work of our hands upon us; yea, the work of our hands establish THOU it.

Revelation 1:5: And from JESUS CHRIST, WHO is the FAITHFUL WITNESS, and the FIRST BEGOTTEN of the dead, and the PRINCE of the kings of the earth. Unto HIM that loved us, and washed us from our sins in HIS own Blood,

Matthew 6:14-15: [14]For if ye forgive men their trespasses, your Heavenly FATHER will also forgive you: [15]But if ye forgive not men their trespasses, neither will your FATHER forgive your trespasses.

Romans 10:3: For they being ignorant of GOD's Righteousness, and going about to establish their own righteousness, have not submitted themselves unto the Righteousness of GOD.

James 4:7: Submit yourselves therefore to GOD. Resist the devil, and he will flee from you.

Ephesians 4:26-27: [26]Be ye angry, and sin not: let not the sun go down upon your wrath: [27]Neither give place to the devil.

John 8:12: Then spake JESUS again unto them, saying, I am the LIGHT of the world: he that followeth ME shall not walk in darkness, but shall have the LIGHT of life.

Matthew 7:22-23: [22]Many will say to ME in that day, LORD, LORD, have we not prophesied in THY Name? And in THY Name have cast out devils? And in THY Name done many wonderful works? [23]And then will I profess unto them, I never knew you: depart from ME, ye that work iniquity.

Deuteronomy 4:24: For the LORD thy GOD is a Consuming FIRE, even a Jealous GOD.

2 Corinthians 11:2: For I am jealous over you with godly jealousy: for I have espoused you to One HUSBAND, that I may present you as a chaste virgin to CHRIST.

James 5:1-5: Go to now, ye rich men, weep and howl for your miseries that shall come upon you. [2]Your riches are corrupted, and your garments are moth eaten. [3]Your gold and silver is cankered; and the rust of them shall be a witness against you, and shall eat your flesh as it were fire. Ye have heaped treasure together for the last days. [4]Behold, the hire of the labourers who have reaped down your fields, which is of you kept back by fraud, crieth: and the cries of them which have reaped are entered into the ears of the LORD of Sabaoth. [5]Ye have lived in pleasure on the earth, and been wanton; ye have nourished your hearts, as in a day of slaughter.

Proverbs 30:5: Every Word of GOD is pure: HE is a SHIELD unto them that put their trust in HIM.

Sat, 7 Jul 2012

The LORD's Words: "I cannot, in any form, bless this overwhelming evil."

Dear Faithful Followers of CHRIST:

To know the future, sometimes you have to look to the past. For instance, if you look at the books of Daniel and Revelation you can find the things foretold hundreds of years ago are now coming about. Now that is so amazing, it is hard to overlook that something foretold so long ago could be coming together with such precision. This is so astounding that the only ones who can deny it are those who, for whatever reason, don't want to believe that we are in the Biblical end times.

For me personally, I was told by the LORD back in March 2009 that I would be doing HIS end times work and to go out and to warn people. Then later December 2009, my pastor gave me a Word from the LORD that I would be an 11th hour worker. Now today, July 2012 I realize there was no way that back in March 2009 that I could have known the events that are now coming about in the world. This tells me how reliable these Words were and how important it is to just keep warning people to get ready and stay ready for the LORD's Return. Within this message are three powerful letters from the LORD telling us to get ready and stay ready for the LORD's Return.

Mark 13:29-30: [29]So ye in like manner, when ye shall see these things come to pass, know that it is nigh, even at the doors. [30]Verily I say unto you, that this generation shall not pass, till all these things be done.

12. Don't Be Like Lot's Wife

"I cannot, in any form, bless this overwhelming evil."

(Words Received from Our LORD by Susan, June 30, 2012)

Yes, WE may begin:

Children, it is I, your LORD Speaking:

The hour is at hand for MY Soon Return. All is ready. I am ready to make MY Triumphant Entry. The hour is nearing for MY Return. Do not doubt MY Words.

I spoke of this event long ago. I foretold MY Coming. I said the things to look for and what would happen prior to MY Return. All these things are falling in line. Everything is lining up with MY Words.

Why do you doubt so? Why do you have so much derision over MY Truths coming to pass? Could it be because you have a tight grip on the things of the world and you do not want to leave this world behind to pursue MY Kingdom, in your heart?

Children, don't be like Lot's wife who looked back to the latter and gave up the better for evil. This same ending will be yours if you continue to cling to this world and MY enemy who holds you captive. What looks normal to you is not. This world holds deceit and lies and goes against MY Truth, MY Words—even the good works of the world are a lie because everything that runs contrary to MY Will, works against MY Kingdom.

This is the deception of the world and MY enemy to lull you into believing that what looks normal and right is true and will save you, but you are clinging to a lie apart from a full surrender to MY Will. All other directions you move in are paved with deceit and treachery. This generation has been easily deceived and pulled away from MY Pure Truth: the Narrow PATH, the True WAY.

So many will be found walking on the broad road of destruction, away from MY Eternal Kingdom, is this true of you? Do you know what direction you are moving in? Are you taking the broad road to destruction or are you walking the straight path to salvation and everlasting life in ME, your LORD and SAVIOR?

There is only ONE Narrow WAY. I am that PATH. All other directions lead to death, eternal damnation, hell everlasting, torment, and great loss. Make your way to MY Narrow PATH quickly.

This is MY Sincere Instruction: Repent of the sin that has filled your life by moving in your own will apart from MY Will. Surrender every aspect of your life to ME—including your future plans. Hand them over and release them to MY Control.

Let ME cover you in MY Blood. I want to clean you in MY Word, wash you clean, prepare you for MY Heavenlies. Open yourself to ME completely and I will fill you with MY SPIRIT. MY SPIRIT will then guide you, lead you into all Truth and by HIS Power you will receive the freedom from sin that you need to be ready for MY Soon Coming.

All is set. All is waiting for you children. I am ready to unite with MY children. I am ready for them to come into MY Presence, to be together, to begin our eternal lives together.

This must be the hour I make MY Great Move as all has turned dark. The world is moving against ME and soon will discover MY Wrath poured out: punishment for overwhelming rejection of its GOD.

Do not be deceived. This hour approaches. It is evil to continue to look to this world for your answers, for your future longings, to cling to a world that only embraces and desires evil and moving apart from GOD. Do you not see this MY children?

I cannot, in any form, bless this overwhelming evil. You dance with the devil if you continue with longings of a future in this world. You excuse your panting after this world in a myriad of ways. All is evil and those who long to live in this world will receive the longings of their hearts, only what is coming to this earth is a departure from what they are imagining.

I will not be mocked! If you pursue this evil world in your heart and all its trimmings then you will enjoy the desires of your heart. It shall come to pass for you as you so desire. So be careful in the lust of the eye after a world that grows colder by the day. Grasp MY Warm Hand and find the salvation of your soul and be rescued from what is coming to this world.

GOD will not be mocked!

Seek the Narrow PATH.

Faithful KING.

STRONGHOLD for dark times.

Mark 13:29: So ye in like manner, when ye shall see these things come to pass, know that it is nigh, even at the doors.

Genesis 19:26: But his wife looked back from behind him, and she became a pillar of salt.

Luke 17:32: Remember Lot's wife.

2 Timothy 4:3: For the time will come when they will not endure sound doctrine; but after their own lusts shall they heap to themselves teachers, having itching ears;

Matthew 7:13: Enter ye in at the strait gate: for wide is the gate, and broad is the way, that leadeth to destruction, and many there be which go in thereat:

Revelation 7:14: And I said unto him, Sir, thou knowest. And he said to me, These are they which came out of great tribulation, and have washed their robes, and made them white in the Blood of the LAMB.

Romans 10:3: For they being ignorant of GOD's righteousness, and going about to establish their own righteousness, have not submitted themselves unto the righteousness of GOD.

Luke 3:16: John answered, saying unto them all, I indeed baptize you with water; but ONE mightier than I cometh, the latchet of WHOSE Shoes I am not worthy to unloose: HE shall baptize you with the HOLY GHOST and with fire:

Matthew 24:12: And because iniquity shall abound, the love of many shall wax cold.

1 John 2:16: For all that is in the world, the lust of the flesh, and the lust of the eyes, and the pride of life, is not of the FATHER, but is of the world.

Galatians 6:7: Be not deceived; GOD is not mocked: for whatsoever a man soweth, that shall he also reap.

If You Are Moving In Your Own Plans ... My Soon Return Will Not Be To Your Liking

Words of the LORD:

"If your eyes are not on ME, you will miss MY Coming"

(Words Received from Our LORD by Susan, July 1, 2012)

Susan it is I, your LORD Speaking:

This is MY Voice. Listen closely:

MY children, the winds are shifting. There is a shift to darkness. The world is growing black. It is turning into a darkened land. The people die from lack of knowledge. They pursue darkness at every turn. All is growing evil. MY Wrath is coming to this world. I want to save you MY children before the hour grows too late.

This hour is coming—a dark day: a day when men will deny ME, their LORD. Tomorrow could be the last day. This is how near MY Coming is. You must stay on high alert: always watching, always anticipating, sensitive to the move of GOD.

Why do I want you on alert? Because just as it was in the days of Noah, so shall it be again: they were eating and drinking, marrying and giving in marriage and so shall it be again. Only those alert, watching, and keeping their lamps full will I allow through MY Door of escape.

This is a serious warning.

MY children do not believe MY Words. They have turned to their own beliefs and ways. They believe watching for MY Return is not essential to their salvation. Without watching for MY Return, you will remain behind when I come for MY bride, MY church. Few want to believe that watching is a requirement of being ready, but without watching you are not looking and you do not have your eyes on ME.

If your eyes are not on ME, you will miss MY Coming and the enemy will distract you and make you his own. Once you belong to MY enemy, destruction is your destination. Few want to ascribe to this Truth. Many want to discount and argue that watching is in MY Will. Only those watching are coming. Only those who pursue ME with a passion are truly MINE. If you are in MY Will than you would be watching MY Every Move and knowing the times you are living in.

If you are moving in your own plans apart from MY Will—than watching for MY Soon Return will not be to your liking. But MY Will is Truth, regardless of the desires and plans of men. Lay down your own plans; surrender your life and plans to ME.

Even MY leaders run their lives apart from ME and are out of step from what I am doing in the world now. Their desire to do their own will, will lead many astray off the path of righteousness and watching for ME and MY Soon Return. Don't be deceived. Even what looks right can be deception from MY enemy who comes as an angel of light. Only by watching for ME is your salvation assured.

Those who move in close and watch MY Every Move will not be disappointed when I lift them out to freedom. All others will be left with great sadness and loss.

Watch MY children, watch for ME. Only those whose spirit is longing for ME will be found ready at MY Coming.

Watch for ME.

The BRIDEGROOM Cometh.

Luke 12:37: Blessed are those servants, whom the LORD when HE cometh shall find watching: verily I say unto you, that HE shall gird HIMSELF, and make them to sit down to meat, and will come forth and serve them.

Matthew 24:42-51: [42]Watch therefore: for ye know not what hour your LORD doth come. [43]But know this, that if the good man of the house had known in what watch the thief would come, he would have watched, and would not have suffered his house to be broken up. [44]Therefore be ye also ready: for in such an hour as ye think not the SON of man cometh.[45]Who then is a faithful and wise servant, whom his lord hath made ruler over his household, to give them meat in due season? [46]Blessed is that servant, whom his lord when he cometh shall find so doing. [47]Verily I say unto you, That he shall make him ruler over all his goods.[48]But and if that evil servant shall say in his heart, My lord delayeth his coming; [49]And shall begin to smite his fellow servants, and to eat and drink with the drunken; [50]The lord of that servant shall come in a day when he looketh not for him, and in an hour that he is not aware of, [51]And shall cut him asunder, and appoint him his portion with the hypocrites: there shall be weeping and gnashing of teeth.

13. Children, Seek Me In All Things

"MY Good Name is tossed about carelessly by callous men like the waves on the sea."

(Words Received from Our LORD by Susan, July 3, 2012)

Daughter, it is I your LORD Speaking. Susan, listen to MY Words:

There are winds of change moving throughout the earth. I am not pleased with men and their rejection of ME. The world is running away from ME. MY children have found other lovers. They are running to and fro looking for answers. But I am the Only True ANSWER!

The answers they are getting will lead them astray. Children, seek ME in all things, for all your ways. Submit your life to ME as time is short and there is very little to make things right with ME. I need a pure bride, one who is not defiled, pure and chaste in all her ways. I cannot take those whose hands remain dirty from the handling of the things of the world. The world is an enmity to ME.

All looks well and fine, but this world and its ways are full of defilement, filth, foul speech. MY Name is slaughtered by all who use it in vain. MY Good Name is tossed about carelessly by callous men like the waves on the sea. Repent of this sin, for no man will face ME without MY Blood Covering and survive it.

Without repentance and submission to ME as your LORD and SAVIOR, all will be cast away for eternity. Don't doubt this message as MY Words speak Truth. I am a GOD of Truth. MY Patience is wearing thin with this evil generation that has such little respect for ME and MY Name.

Soon, I will dispense with the evil that plagues this earth, but not before I punish those who have turned against ME, mock ME, and ruthlessly despise MY Laws and Commandments.

Grace has not dispensed with MY Commandments. It only enables men to live successfully with them. Children you must still follow MY Ways. How else will you know the Way of purity? Submit to ME fully. Receive the outpouring of MY SPIRIT and HE will lead you down the pathway of righteousness and deliverance.

No man can conquer sin apart from the impartation of MY SPIRIT. Only by the SPIRIT in full measure do you obtain the power to walk in MY Ways and Laws. Receive MY SPIRIT fully, experience the covering of MY Blood, and be empowered to walk in Truth, Freedom, and MY Saving Grace. It is yours…Deliverance is yours…Freedom from sin is yours.

Come to the end of "self" and place your life in MY Hands. Be free of the temptations of evil. Walk daily with ME. Peace and sound mind are yours. Leave the oppression of living apart from GOD, your CREATOR, MAKER. Come back into MY Loving Arms.

I am waiting to save you, preserve you for MYSELF for eternity.

Refresh in MY Springs of LIVING WATERS

I am your LORD and SAVIOR.

Blessed REDEEMER.

EMANUEL.

2 Timothy 4:3: For the time will come when they will not endure sound doctrine; but after their own lusts shall they heap to themselves teachers, having itching ears;

Daniel 12:4: But thou, O Daniel, shut up the words, and seal the book, even to the time of the end: many shall run to and fro, and knowledge shall be increased.

John 12:25: He that loveth his life shall lose it; and he that hateth his life in this world shall keep it unto life eternal.

Leviticus 19:12: And ye shall not swear by MY Name falsely, neither shalt thou profane the Name of thy GOD: I am the LORD.

Hebrews 10:19: Having therefore, brethren, boldness to enter into the holiest by the Blood of JESUS,

Hebrews 10:29: Of how much sorer punishment, suppose ye, shall he be thought worthy, who hath trodden underfoot the SON of GOD, and hath counted the Blood of the covenant, wherewith he was sanctified, an unholy thing, and hath done despite unto the SPIRIT of grace?

Romans 6:15: What then? Shall we sin, because we are not under the law, but under grace? GOD forbid.

Revelation 12:17: And the dragon was wroth with the woman, and went to make war with the remnant of her seed, which keep the commandments of GOD, and have the testimony of JESUS CHRIST.

Matthew 19:17: And HE said unto him, Why callest thou ME good? There is none good but ONE, that is, GOD: but if thou wilt enter into life, keep the commandments.

Hebrews 10:16: This is the covenant that I will make with them after those days, saith the LORD, I will put MY laws into their hearts, and in their minds will I write them;

My Lukewarm Church Will Be Cast Away

The LORD's Words: "Now is the hour to make things right between US."

The LORD's Words for Today (Posted at www.End-Times-Prophecy.Com)

Words of the LORD:

"MY lukewarm church will be cast away because they chose to seek intimacy with MY enemy while attempting to handle the Holy."

(Words Received from Our LORD by Susan, July 7, 2012)

Daughter I will give you Words and WE can begin:

These are MY Words. Do not doubt. Children, it is your LORD from up above. I have Words for you today.

The world will experience a closure to life as it has been known. With MY Protective Hand, I have been keeping back the troubles from the earth you are now seeing that are manifesting because of men's disobedience and rejection of GOD.

Soon, I will lift MY true followers and true church away from this evil world to safety. Are you ready to go? Do you want to come with those who will be joining ME at MY Marriage Supper Table? This is a grand day, a time of celebration, longing fulfilled.

MY blessed children will be joining ME to exchange our joy, laughter, and love. What a time of happiness for MY bride as WE come together for all eternity. You can join us. Unite with ME, your GOD. This is MY Desire for you, to bring you wholeness, deliver you from the evil to come.

Children, you cannot make peace with ME, your GOD apart from MY Blood Covering, MY HOLY SPIRIT in all HIS Fullness, and without a humble and complete submission to ME with repentance of your past sins. This is MY Requirement to salvation.

Dear children, come to ME now! Lay your life before ME. Focus your sight on ME. I am the ONE True WAY to safety from the evil that is descending on the earth. There is no other route to safety. Run into MY Arms of safety, peace, and life everlasting. Cling to ME. Come close, turn from your evil and seek ME in all your ways.

There are no answers to this world lost in hopelessness. What looks right and true is a trap laid by MY enemy to entice you away from ME—the ONE, True ESCAPE ROUTE. He wants to send you to hell. He wants to lead you astray. He wants to take your life from you, to destroy you.

All that you see in the world is deception hatched by MY enemy for your demise. Many fall into this trap, more are deceived then saved. Few find the Narrow PATH. Only a few make it into MY Arms of safety. Don't be deceived as others would have you believe differently. They want you to believe that you can have both the ways of the world and ME also. This is a lie from the pit of hell.

MY lukewarm church will be cast away because they chose to seek intimacy with MY enemy while attempting to handle the Holy. The two cannot mix. What place does darkness have in MY Kingdom?

Stop and consider what choices you are making. Your pursuit of the world while pursuing ME causes you to be double minded and unstable in all your ways—watch out as your footing is unsure and MY enemy is looking for a way to come between us. Soon, I will leave you to your pursuits of the world when I come to pull MY true church out to safety.

Choices must be made. Will you choose for ME, your CREATOR or to run with MY enemy? He is only too eager to take you away from ME. So come in close to ME and I will provide you with shelter from the storm. Lay your life before ME—let ME take your life and I will use it for MY Glory and to reach others who are drowning in the lies of the world.

The hour is short. Come quickly to MY Saving Grace. Let ME sanctify and purify you, make you ready for MY Kingdom.

This is GOD…The ONLY GOD…SAVIOR of all

I am the ONE WHO holds all the answers to the universe.

Search no more, I hold ALL Truth.

Rest assured, I hold the keys to life.

FATHER…SON…HOLY SPIRIT.

TRIUNE GOD.

Acts 20:28: Take heed therefore unto yourselves, and to all the flock, over the which the HOLY GHOST hath made you overseers, to feed the church of GOD, which HE hath purchased with HIS OWN Blood.

Romans 10:3: For they being ignorant of GOD's righteousness, and going about to establish their own righteousness, have not submitted themselves unto the righteousness of GOD.

Mark 1:15: And saying, The time is fulfilled, and the kingdom of GOD is at hand: repent ye, and believe the gospel.

Mark 2:17: When JESUS heard it, HE saith unto them, They that are whole have no need of the physician, but they that are sick: I came not to call the righteous, but sinners to repentance.

Mark 6:12: And they went out, and preached that men should repent.

John 10:10: The thief cometh not, but for to steal, and to kill, and to destroy: I am come that they might have life, and that they might have it more abundantly.

2 Corinthians 6:14: Be ye not unequally yoked together with unbelievers: for what fellowship hath righteousness with unrighteousness? And what communion hath light with darkness?

James 1:8: A double minded man is unstable in all his ways.

James 4:8: Draw nigh to GOD, and HE will draw nigh to you. Cleanse your hands, ye sinners; and purify your hearts, ye double minded.

14. Nothing Can Stop What I Have Ordained

Words of the LORD:

"Do you really believe that apart from MY Guiding Hand that this world will rebound to peace and bounty?"

(Words Received from Our LORD by Susan, July 9, 2012)

Susan, listen to MY Words, write them down:

I am approaching the earth. Nothing can stop what I have ordained. The hour is approaching. Too many still believe that MY Words are not true. Too many think that MY Book is a fable and that evil man will not have a day of reckoning with his GOD. This couldn't be the furthest thing from the truth. Even now, I am beginning to pour out MY Retribution over this earth, MY Punishment for blatant sin and disobedience of mankind.

Although I am a Patient GOD, MY Promises will come to pass just in the way I have given them. MY Word is True. Read MY Word. See that all that I said would happen is happening. I am true to MY Word.

Children, do you not see the destruction coming to the world? Can you not see that this world is in trouble? Do you really believe that apart from MY Guiding Hand that this world will rebound to peace and bounty? Trouble is coming children, the trouble I described in MY Book. It is coming. Don't doubt MY Word.

I gave these Words to prepare your heart, to make you ready, to bring you unto MYSELF so that you can avoid the wrath to follow. MY church was not meant for wrath. This is not her legacy. She will be caught up and protected, shielded from the tyranny that lies ahead.

The lukewarm, idolaters, rebellious, blasphemers, and sexually immoral will remain behind to taste the outcome of a world gone mad, bereft of its GOD's Hand of protection and guidance. The world will witness life apart from MY Love and Devotion.

Step into the power of MY HOLY SPIRIT. Make a full surrender to ME of your life. Only then can I fill you and bring into MY Complete Likeness, only then can you successfully conquer sin and be made HOLY without wrinkle, blemish, or stain: ready for MY Coming and rapture of the bride to safety.

These are MY instructions. Repent of your sin. Lay your life down. Give ME a complete surrender. Withhold nothing from ME. Give ME everything you are and everything you have. Let ME take your life over. Let ME bring your ashes into MY Beauty. Until you do this, you are apart from ME and you belong to MY enemy. He is your lord and master. He controls you and you do what pleases him against MY Kingdom, MY Will, MY Ways. You are working against ME no matter what you think and what it looks like—you are in opposition to ME.

So think this over carefully. Do you want to be outside MY Kingdom for eternity, apart from your GOD, your MAKER? This is where you remain until you surrender your all to ME from a repentant, humbled heart.

There is little time remaining before I make MY Moves and pull MY people out to safety. Be among these peculiar people: those who surrender all to their GOD and walk away from the ways of the world.

I await your decision. The hour presses forward. Don't be caught without MY Blood Covering.

I am a GOD of Truth. There is no other Truth.

I am the Great TRUTH BEARER.

ALMIGHTY GOD.

Psalm 95:11: Unto whom I sware in MY wrath that they should not enter into MY rest.

Ezekiel 7:19: They shall cast their silver in the streets, and their gold shall be removed: their silver and their gold shall not be able to deliver them in the day of the wrath of the LORD: they shall not satisfy their souls, neither fill their bowels: because it is the stumbling block of their iniquity.

Nahum 1:2: GOD is jealous, and the LORD revengeth; the LORD revengeth, and is furious; the LORD will take vengeance on HIS adversaries, and HE reserveth wrath for HIS enemies.

1 Thessalonians 5:9: For GOD hath not appointed us to wrath, but to obtain salvation by our LORD JESUS CHRIST,

2 Timothy 3:1-4: [1]This know also, that in the last days perilous times shall come. [2] For men shall be lovers of their own selves, covetous, boasters, proud, blasphemers, disobedient to parents, unthankful, unholy, [3] Without natural affection, trucebreakers, false accusers, incontinent, fierce, despisers of those that are good, [4] Traitors, heady, high minded, lovers of pleasures more than lovers of GOD;

2 Corinthians 3:18: But we all, with open face beholding as in a glass the glory of the LORD, are changed into the same image from glory to glory, even as by the SPIRIT of the LORD.

Isaiah 61:3: To appoint unto them that mourn in Zion, to give unto them beauty for ashes, the oil of joy for mourning, the garment of praise for the spirit of heaviness; that they might be called trees of righteousness, the planting of the LORD, that he might be glorified.

1 John 2:15: Love not the world, neither the things that are in the world. If any man love the world, the love of the FATHER is not in him.

Revelation 19:15: And out of HIS Mouth goeth a sharp sword, that with it HE should smite the nations: and HE shall rule them with a rod of iron: and HE treadeth the winepress of the fierceness and wrath of ALMIGHTY GOD.

Now Is The Hour To Make Things Right Between Us

Words of the LORD:

"Now is the hour to make things right between US."

(Words Received from Our LORD by Susan, July 12, 2012)

Susan, it is your LORD. Listen carefully, as I give you Words:

There is a day and an hour that MY people will not listen to reason. They will turn away from what is right and do what they want in their own sinful hearts.

This hour has come.

Those who choose against ME rise up and boldly shake their fist at ME to let ME know, through defiance, they will do whatever they will do, whatever is in their heart, and not follow ME. The people have gone mad with evil, rebellion, and witchcraft. Their hearts rule over them. They work against their GOD. They blaspheme and rise up to do their own will. They shake the fist and say: "I will be MY own god…I will rule myself…I will have no one tell me how to live."

These are MY rebellious children, who cover the earth. They are thick in number—countless numbers who do their own bidding and follow their god, MY enemy. He rules their heart. They take orders from him. Though they do it unknowingly, he is their master and they pull down many as they go through life.

Yea, even MY leaders who lead many, mislead, drag MY people astray by the doctrines of men and devils; this, because they refuse to surrender their all to ME—they refuse to repent and surrender. They want to do things their way and not in MY Will.

How is it that you can know MY Will? Only by a surrender of the heart and your own will and plans. You must be willing to lay it all before ME. This is the only way to MY Salvation. There is no other safe path—you may walk in a myriad of directions, but there is only One Safe Path. I am the Narrow ROAD to Truth. I need you to surrender your all to ME from a humbled, repentant heart. There is no other way by which a man can be saved except by MY Blood Covering received through a complete surrender to ME. Only through a full surrender will you then receive MY HOLY SPIRIT in all His fullness to fill your lamp oil. It is by HIS Power that you can live the life I set before you to live in: purity, humility, and without sin. This is how MY children can be set free and made ready for MY Coming to bring them out to safety.

Don't let anyone deceive you—there is no other way. Lay your life down before ME. Cry out to ME that you want ME as your LORD and MASTER. Then, I can bring you to MY Salvation and save you from the wrath to come. Now is the hour to make things right between US. Let ME clear the way to your salvation; give you safe passage to MY Heavenlies. I am willing. MY Blood is free for the asking.

This is your SAVIOR, WHO pleads with you. Seek MY Salvation. Get to know ME in deep intimacy. Your time is running short.

I Love you,

Heaven's LAMB.

Galatians 5:19-21: [19] Now the works of the flesh are manifest, which are these; Adultery, fornication, uncleanness, lasciviousness, [20] Idolatry, witchcraft, hatred, variance, emulations, wrath, strife, seditions, heresies, [21] Envyings, murders, drunkenness, revellings, and such like: of the which I tell you before, as I have also told you in time past, that they which do such things shall not inherit the kingdom of GOD.

Galatians 1:14: And profited in the Jews' religion above many my equals in mine own nation, being more exceedingly zealous of the traditions of my fathers.

Matthew 15:9: But in vain they do worship ME, teaching for doctrines the commandments of men.

Ephesians 4:14: That we henceforth be no more children, tossed to and fro, and carried about with every wind of doctrine, by the sleight of men, and cunning craftiness, whereby they lie in wait to deceive;

John 14:6: JESUS saith unto him, I am the WAY, the TRUTH, and the LIFE: no man cometh unto the FATHER, but by ME.

Galatians 5:16: This I say then, Walk in the SPIRIT, and ye shall not fulfil the lust of the flesh.Date: Sat, 21 Jul 2012 11:22:15 -0400

"You are mesmerized by the world and all its false hope."

The LORD's Words for Today (Posted at www.End-Times-Prophecy.Com)

If You Only Knew How Close My Coming Is…

Words of the LORD:

"Let ME find you awake at MY Coming!"

(Words Received from Our LORD by Susan, July 17, 2012)

The time is drawing near for MY Return to earth. It is closing in. There are only a few really paying attention. I have been clear in all ways what to look for. I have put forth signs to watch for. I have given many signs to know that MY Coming is soon. Yet MY Word is disregarded and men have chosen to reject ME, their LORD. This is what they prefer.

I am always clear in MY Writings, MY Word—all Scripture is inspired by the HOLY SPIRIT. HE is the ONE WHO breathes life into every Word. MY Word is life. It speaks Truth and MY Words are everlasting. This is why men can turn to MY Word and find all Truth, Guidance, and all the Answers they need to live in this life.

There is no other source that speaks absolute Truth for mankind to know and understand what GOD expects of them in this life. This is why MY enemy tries hard to lead men astray from MY Words of Truth. Stay in MY Words: MY Words are Gold, Precious Jewels of Truth and Knowledge and Power—the same Power of MY SPIRIT that strengthens you to battle sin and MY enemy. He cannot withstand MY children who have built up their faith by reading MY Word. There is Power in Knowledge and Truth.

Children, if you only knew how close MY Coming is, you would awaken from your slumber—you would not neglect MY Word and you would be strong in MY Truth through the Power of MY SPIRIT. It is only by MY SPIRIT that you can conquer sin and the affliction of MY enemy in your life. I want you to be whole and made ready for MY Return.

So awaken to Truth—read MY Word, Surrender your ALL to ME. Follow hard after your LORD. Seek ME at every turn. Let ME guide you. Surrender your life over to ME—FULL SURRENDER! Leave nothing behind. Place your entire life in MY Hands. Let ME Take your life and create sweet music. Let ME Write beautiful music onto your heart. Let ME Refresh your spirit by Breathing new life into your spirit. Your oil lamp will be filled and your focus will be on ME.

Do not take your eyes off of ME: neither look to the right or the left. I need to be your complete focus. The hour is coming when men will not endure truth—they only want what their wicked hearts want to hear.

MY enemy reigns in terror across the land—there is only one direction to move in to find safety: toward ME—your LORD and SAVIOR. There is no other answer. Seek MY Face while I can still be found. You have limited time to make your choice. Let ME find you awake at MY Coming. MY bride is bright-eyed and watching for her GROOM, her LORD.

Make preparation. Get ready. Clean yourself up in MY Blood. This is a serious hour as the world turns to reject its GOD. Don't be caught unawares. Awaken to Truth, MY Truth. It is available through the Pages of MY Book.

"I AM" has Spoken Truth

Seek ME in ALL your ways

Prepare for MY Return

2 Timothy 3:16: All scripture is given by inspiration of GOD, and is profitable for doctrine, for reproof, for correction, for instruction in righteousness:

Psalms 119:72: The law of THY mouth is better unto me than thousands of gold and silver.

Psalms 119:127: Therefore I love THY Commandments above gold; yea, above fine gold.

Job 33:4: The SPIRIT of GOD hath made me, and the breath of the ALMIGHTY hath given me life.

Matthew 19:29: And every one that hath forsaken houses, or brethren, or sisters, or father, or mother, or wife, or children, or lands, for MY Name's sake, shall receive an hundredfold, and shall inherit everlasting life.

Matthew 24:12:And because iniquity shall abound, the love of many shall wax cold.

Hosea 4:6: MY people are destroyed for lack of knowledge: because thou hast rejected knowledge, I will also reject thee, that thou shalt be no priest to ME: seeing thou hast forgotten the law of thy GOD, I will also forget thy children.

Psalm 112:7: He shall not be afraid of evil tidings: his heart is fixed, trusting in the LORD.

Mark 7:9: And HE said unto them, Full well ye reject the Commandment of GOD, that ye may keep your own tradition.

Hebrews 10:38: Now the just shall live by faith: but if any man draws back, MY Soul shall have no pleasure in him.

Psalms 40:3:And HE hath put a new song in my mouth, even praise unto our GOD: many shall see it, and fear, and shall trust in the LORD.

When You Reject My Spirit And His Call On Your Life, You Endanger Your Soul

Words of the LORD:

"When you reject MY SPIRIT and HIS Call on your life, you endanger your soul."

(Words Received from Our LORD by Susan, July 18, 2012)

Daughter, I will Speak Words to you, write them down:

Children, it is I, your LORD—I am the Great "I AM"—there is no other like ME—I am the BEGINNING and the END—I am the BRIGHT and MORNING STAR.

The world is in trouble. MY children, it falters, it wanes. Many do not see it. Many more are beginning to see the changes coming about—great changes. Men are engaging in evil acts: men running apart from GOD. So few see the Truth, so few will be ready when I come: only those who really are watching—all others who believe themselves ready, will come up short, and they will be cut down as MY enemy resumes his position of ruler over this evil world. He rules the hearts of wicked men who run apart from GOD.

Men are covering the earth, who are outside MY Will: men who believe themselves MY followers, neither grasp or understand MY Truth. Their lips lie and distort MY Truth at every turn. They turn MY Truth into heresies and lies to free themselves of their guilt of following after the things of the world. The world pleases them, so they must alter MY Truth in order to engage with MY enemy. Dark days lie ahead for those who think they can have this world and MY Kingdom both.

Their hearts beat fast for the world as they turn to handle MY Truth. The two cannot mix. You must not engage in this evil. Turn your life over to ME. Make ME your LORD and MASTER. I will pull you away from the world by the Life-changing Power of MY SPIRIT. You cannot make this change apart from GOD: MY SPIRIT; MY Power; MY Will for your life; and MY Blood Covering.

There is no power in the flesh. Many try to operate out of the flesh and they come up short, more frustrated than when they started. There is a reason for this: sin cannot be conquered in the flesh apart from the Healing Hand of GOD: only by MY Power can you do what I Will for your life. All you can do is come to ME with a broken spirit: humbled and hungry for MY Salvation and Deliverance. Then, and only then, as you pray from a heart of humility, brokenness, repentance for your life of sin, can I step in and assume MY Role as your ETERNAL PARTNER, SAVIOR, DELIVERER.

Those who come to ME with pride, disbelief, lack of faith will not hear MY Message and come in danger of blaspheming MY SPIRIT. When you reject MY SPIRIT and HIS Call on your life you endanger your soul. It is MY SPIRIT WHO Draws you to MY Salvation and Blood Covering—without which, you cannot stand before US. Your acts of treason, rebellion while in your mortal body, will be judged guilty and your punishment will be eternal hell: separation from GOD and ALL MY Glory.

This is a serious hour. Serious decisions need to be made. Will you persist in your rejection of MY SPIRIT's Calling to MY Blood-bought Salvation? Each day brings you closer to the possibility of losing your last chance to make things right with your GOD and once you pass that point, your loss will be eternal.

Don't risk losing your salvation and place in MY Kingdom. Too many have gone before you who now have eternal regrets that cannot be undone. You decide. Are you coming with ME when I Rescue MY bride or will you be left to face MY enemy or worse: be lost in sudden destruction?

Time is wasting. What is more important than your eternal soul?

When we stand face-to-face - you will either realize the BLESSINGS OF FOLLOWING ME OR the TERROR OF BEING SENT AWAY FOR ETERNITY.

MY Words are TRUTH.

TRUTH has Spoken.

Revelation 22:16: I JESUS have sent mine angel to testify unto you these things in the churches. I am the ROOT and the OFFSPRING of David, and the BRIGHT and MORNING STAR.

Proverbs 26:11: As a dog returneth to his vomit, so a fool returneth to his folly.

2 Peter 2:22: But it is happened unto them according to the true proverb, The dog is turned to his own vomit again; and the sow that was washed to her wallowing in the mire.

Mark 3:29: But he that shall blaspheme against the HOLY GHOST hath never forgiveness, but is in danger of eternal damnation.

1 John 5:6: This is he that came by water and blood, even JESUS CHRIST; not by water only, but by water and blood. And it is the SPIRIT that beareth witness, because the SPIRIT is Truth.

John 6:44: No man can come to ME, except the FATHER which hath sent ME Draw him: and I will raise him up at the last day.

Romans 8:5: For they that are after the flesh do mind the things of the flesh; but they that are after the SPIRIT the things of the SPIRIT.

1 Thessalonians 5:3: For when they shall say, Peace and safety; then sudden destruction cometh upon them, as travail upon a woman with child; and they shall not escape.

15. Take Off Your Blinders - Open Your Eyes

Words of the LORD:

"You are mesmerized by the world and all its false hope."

(Words Received from Our LORD by Susan, July 19, 2012)

Daughter, it is time to begin again:

MY children: your GOD knows you. I know MY children. I know every detail of your life. I know the way you suffer. I know what makes you happy. I know when you get up and when you go down at night. Nothing gets by ME, children. All is seen by ME, GOD.

I am a GOD WHO is from everlasting to everlasting. MY Presence is always near. I consume the earth. MY SPACE occupies everything. I am ALL CONSUMING. There is no getting away from GOD, though men try, nothing is hidden from MY Sight. I know what makes men think the way they think. I know what men will do before they do it. ALL is known by ME: there are no secrets from GOD.

Come to ME in this last, great hour. I know who is mine. I know who I Call. I Know who will answer MY Call. I Know who will not answer and who rejects his GOD. I know who is hell-bound and heaven-bound. This is all known by ME. I know who MY eternal heaven-bound children are—MY bride eternal. She is lovely in all her ways because she possesses MY SPIRIT. She has laid her life down before ME, given ME her all and WE have taken up residence in her spirit—MY SPIRIT indwells her completely. She walks as I want her to walk—in MY Will for her life. She is MY sweet bride—the light remaining in this dark world.

Be among these chosen people. I have chosen MY people from the foundation of the earth. This is MY chosen bride. You may step into her shoes: assume your place with ME for eternity, to rule and reign with GOD. Does MY Word not speak it?

I Speak and MY Word does not change. Don't miss this hour that is coming for MY beautiful bride to assume her position with ME for eternity as I place her by MY Side. Regrets will be great for those left and lost after MY bride comes out with ME, saved from the wrath that is portioned to the earth.

Listen to these Words children: all is changing—the world is becoming a harsh place to dwell. Truth is diminishing. Evil man in conjunction with MY enemy is blocking MY Truth and thus darkness is ruling. Do you not see this? Can you not see the darkness coming over the earth?

Take off your blinders—open your eyes. You are mesmerized by the world and all its false hope. You believe there is a long life ahead—but this is a scheme of the enemy to keep you from Truth, to keep you from preparing yourself: washing in MY Blood and MY Word—cleaning yourself in MY Truth. This plan of deception was devised by MY enemy long ago. Don't fall into his trap for you. Awaken to MY Truth. Pull yourself out of this slumber you are in. Come to terms with what is happening around you. Prepare for MY Coming!

I do not want you to remain behind for the evil that is at the door. Bury yourself in MY Word. Dig deep, find Truth, seek Truth. It is there for the taking, for the asking! MY Light is available. Ask to be filled by MY SPIRIT, enlightened by HIS Truth. Let ME fill your heart, make you ready.

Ask ME, children! Ask! I cry out to you—Ask of ME!

This is GOD Pleading—don't miss MY Coming Glory!

I AM THE COMING GLORY

Ecclesiastes 12:14: For GOD shall bring every work into judgment, with every secret thing, whether it be good, or whether it be evil.

Jeremiah 23:23-24: Am I a GOD at hand, saith the LORD, and not a GOD afar off? [24]Can any hide himself in secret places that I shall not see him? Saith the LORD. Do not I fill heaven and earth? Saith the LORD.

1 John 4:13: Hereby know we that we dwell in HIM, and HE in us, because HE hath given us of HIS SPIRIT.

Matthew 22:14: For many are called, but few are chosen.

John 15:16: Ye have not chosen ME, but I have chosen you, and ordained you, that ye should go and bring forth fruit, and that your fruit should remain: that whatsoever ye shall ask of the FATHER in MY Name, HE may give it you.

2 Thessalonians 2:13: But we are bound to give thanks always to GOD for you, brethren beloved of the LORD, because GOD hath from the beginning chosen you to salvation through sanctification of the SPIRIT and belief of the Truth:

Revelation 17:14: These shall make war with the LAMB, and the LAMB shall overcome them: for HE is LORD of lords, and KING of kings: and they that are with HIM are called, and chosen, and faithful.

1 Corinthians 3:18-19: Let no man deceive himself. If any man among you seemeth to be wise in this world, let him become a fool,

that he may be wise. [19]For the wisdom of this world is foolishness with GOD. For it is written, HE taketh the wise in their own craftiness.

2 Timothy 2:10: Therefore I endure all things for the elect's sakes, that they may also obtain the salvation which is in CHRIST JESUS, with eternal glory.

2 Thessalonians 2:12: That they all might be damned who believed not the Truth, but had pleasure in unrighteousness.

Date: Wed, 8 Aug 2012 01:59:17 -0400

The LORD's Words: "Blind Faith causes MY enemy to tremble."

The LORD's Words for Today (Posted at www.End-Times-Prophecy.Com)

Dear Faithful Followers of CHRIST:

Matthew 7:22-23: [22]Many will say to me in that day, LORD, LORD, have we not prophesied in THY Name? And in THY Name have cast out devils? And in THY Name done many wonderful works? [23]And then will I profess unto them, I never knew you: depart from ME, ye that work iniquity. This group the LORD is making reference to in Matthew 7:22-23 are engaging in SPIRIT-filled activities—prophesying, casting out demons, and doing wonderful works. Could these be the five virgins with half their lamps full—some of the SPIRIT but not all of the oil so that they are turned away by the LORD? They have some oil because you cannot do these things listed in this scripture without the HOLY SPIRIT, but it isn't enough because they are rejected by CHRIST ultimately. But the key of this verse is when the LORD says: "I never knew you," to which the people are ordered to depart, rejected.

GOD doesn't just want our cheap attempts to impress HIM, HE wants to "KNOW" us. How can you know GOD? Read your bible, pray (talk to GOD); get to KNOW HIM by spending time with HIM. Then, when HE Returns—HE will acknowledge you and you won't be a stranger to HIM.

16. They Devise A God In Their Own Mind

Words of the LORD:

"Your rote and dead worship does not impress ME."

(Words Received from Our LORD by Susan, August 3, 2012)

MY child, it is I, your LORD. WE can begin:

Children, this is your GOD Speaking. I have Words for you...so few are listening...so few want to hear ME. It is just as MY Word said it would be, like the time of Noah.

The day is coming for MY Return. I am looking for an attentive bride. One who longs for MY Appearing. MY Word is clear and does not change.

For those who drink of the lukewarm waters, there will be much sadness. You will not be taken when I come for MY bride. She stands apart from the rest—eager for her BRIDEGROOM'S Return. This is the one that I am coming for—the church that worships and loves its GOD wholeheartedly and without reservation, embracing MY Truths, MY Word, MY Ways. All others seek a god who meets their own criteria, satisfies their longings for the world so they can touch and handle the ways of the world.

They believe they know ME, but they devise a god in their own mind's they want to worship and it is not the ONE, True Living GOD—it is a god they have constructed to meet their selfish needs and it is an idol, a god who is imaginary, a god who allows them to love the world and its wicked ways. This is MY lukewarm church—the stagnant pool: lukewarm in all its ways...a stench, a foul stench to ME. She will be left standing at the altar when I come for MY true bride.

Children, consider your choices and the decisions you make. Are you coming out with ME to return to an eternal home or will you remain cool toward ME and stay behind? You embrace a dying world. She is dying and this is what you have chosen over the ONE TRUE GOD: Eternal ALPHA and OMEGA.

Your senses have been numbed to Truth: you can't hear it, see it, smell it, or taste it. You are deaf, dumb, and blind to righteousness, holiness, and MY Way Everlasting. You have given up BEAUTY for ashes. Ashes you want and ashes you will have—soon this world will turn to ashes and it will be too late for MY lukewarm church to turn back to BEAUTY because I will have already departed with MY one, true bride, MY church: humble followers who follow their GOD with blind faith and fervent love and desire for ME and MY Ways.

Lukewarm church: time is running out for you. Your rote and dead worship does not impress ME. Your lack of repentance and remorse over sin shows ME the place you hold for ME in your heart. When I am first place, then and only then, will your oil lamp be full. Does MY Word not speak this?

O' tepid church: church who has eyes for everyone but ME, wake now before it is too late. Open your blind eyes; unstop your deaf ears—come to the end of yourself. You will have an eternity to regret these moments if you don't turn back to ME!

HEAVEN'S ETERNAL FLAME

Luke 17:26-30: [26]And as it was in the days of Noah, so shall it be also in the days of the SON of man. [27]They did eat, they drank, they married wives, they were given in marriage, until the day that Noah entered into the ark, and the flood came, and destroyed them all. ²⁸Likewise also as it was in the days of Lot; they did eat, they drank, they bought, they sold, they planted, they builded; ²⁹But the same day that Lot went out of Sodom it rained fire and brimstone from heaven, and destroyed them all. ³⁰Even thus shall it be in the day when the SON of man is revealed.

2 Timothy 4:8: Henceforth there is laid up for me a crown of righteousness, which the LORD, the Righteous JUDGE, shall give me at that day: and not to me only, but unto all them also that love HIS Appearing.

John 4:24: GOD is a SPIRIT: and they that worship HIM must worship HIM in SPIRIT and in Truth.

Romans 1:25: Who changed the Truth of GOD into a lie, and worshipped and served the creature more than the CREATOR, WHO is blessed forever. Amen.

Revelation 3:16: So then because thou art lukewarm, and neither cold nor hot, I will spue thee out of MY Mouth.

Revelation 3:18: I counsel thee to buy of ME gold tried in the fire, that thou mayest be rich; and white raiment, that thou mayest be clothed, and that the shame of thy nakedness do not appear; and anoint thine eyes with eyesalve, that thou mayest see.

Isaiah 61:3: To appoint unto them that mourn in Zion, to give unto them beauty for ashes, the oil of joy for mourning, the garment of praise for the spirit of heaviness; that they might be called trees of righteousness, the planting of the LORD, that HE might be glorified.

17. Very Few Are Watching Or Waiting On Me

Words of the LORD:

"Only MY Blood can set a man free."

(Words Received from Our LORD by Susan, August 4, 2012)

I will give you Words now:

Soon children, soon MY Coming is approaching. Very few are watching or waiting on ME with earnest expectation. The people cannot take their eyes off of the world and their lust for the world consumes them. This is more important than their GOD. They cannot trade their time with the world for time for time with their MAKER, the ONE WHO gives them life every day.

I, GOD, am coming for the ones who know ME, who spend time getting to know their GOD. This is who I am ready to bring to MY Side. She is MY bride: those who follow after their GOD with longing hearts. These are the ones I have prepared an Eternal Home for, the ones I am bringing with ME when I come to gather MY Own.

Are you coming? Do you want to be among these special children, the bride eternal? You may become part of her. I extend this invitation to come out of the world, set apart for ME, your KING.

It is not too late—come now before ME in total surrender with deep remorse over your past sins. I can clean you in MY Blood, wipe your stains away. It is MINE to do, no one else can wipe away your debt, your sin debt to GOD. Only I can erase your past mistakes with the Blood I shed on a cruel cross.

This was MY Work, MY Accomplishment to triumph over evil and its hold on mankind. This is MY Gift to mankind: freedom from eternal oppression and punishment. Be freed of the sin chains that bind you. Come to ME in humble submission. Let ME See in your heart that you want ME to be your LORD and MASTER. There is no other safe route to freedom. Only MY Blood can set a man free.

I am waiting, but time is short. So turn and make things right with your GOD as I have cleared a way for you to go. Have I not parted the seas for MY people? Have I not provided a way for MY servant on the ark? Have I not laid MY OWN LIFE down in humble surrender to an evil cross? This I did so that you might have eternal life and life more abundantly.

The hour is now to choose. Choose your GOD, WHO Died for you. There is nothing greater than intimacy with GOD. Though you seek and search, you will not find that which I offer to you freely anywhere else. Discover this Truth now before it is too late.

Shake yourself free from the evil of the tyranny of sin. MY Coming is closing in...

Eternal LORD and MASTER.

1 John 2:16: For all that is in the world, the lust of the flesh, and the lust of the eyes, and the pride of life, is not of the FATHER, but is of the world.

Genesis 2:7: And the LORD GOD formed man of the dust of the ground, and breathed into his nostrils the breath of life; and man became a living soul.

Matthew 22:1-5: And Jesus answered and spake unto them again by parables, and said, [2]The kingdom of heaven is like unto a certain king, which made a marriage for his son, ³And sent forth his servants to call them that were bidden to the wedding: and they would not come. ⁴Again, he sent forth other servants, saying, Tell them which are bidden, Behold, I have prepared my dinner: my oxen and my fatlings are killed, and all things are ready: come unto the marriage. ⁵But they made light of it, and went their ways, one to his farm, another to his merchandise:

Ephesians 5:27: That he might present it to himself a glorious church, not having spot, or wrinkle, or any such thing; but that it should be holy and without blemish.

Romans 8:12: Therefore, brethren, we are debtors, not to the flesh, to live after the flesh.

Romans 5:18: ¹⁸Therefore as by the offence of one judgment came upon all men to condemnation; even so by the righteousness of one the free gift came upon all men unto justification of life.

Surrender All From A Heart Turned To Me Out Of Blind Faith

Words of the LORD:

"Blind Faith causes MY enemy to tremble."

People wanted notes from the conference speakers from our recent End Times Prophecy Conference. I received this message from the LORD for the attendees of the recent End Times Prophecy Conference held July 27-28, 2012 and I also want to share it now with others. The LORD told me the words HE wanted emphasized at the conference were "Blind Faith." –GOD bless you, Susan

MY Coming is near—even at the door. They need to prepare themselves. Wash in MY Blood. Be vigilant watchers—tell others. Warn them about the chip. There needs to be repentance. Focus on ME. There are answers nowhere else. All doors are closing that leads to Truth. Only ONE Door remains—walk through it before it is too late.

Come to ME for a filling of the SPIRIT. Come now—don't delay. Delay may put you in danger of total loss. Let ME overhaul your heart. Make it clean by the washing of MY Word. There are no other solutions. I am the STRAIGHT PATH. I am the LIGHT, the TRUTH.

Blind Faith is the only way to walk with GOD—Surrender ALL from a heart turned to ME out of Blind Faith. Operate in Blind Faith and you will move mountains. You will fly in the heavenlies and soar on wings like eagles…soaring to new heights.

Blind Faith causes MY enemy to tremble. "Blind" because you come to ME blindly not knowing what the outcome of your faith will be: "faith" with anticipated hope that your pursuit of GOD will be GOD's Perfect Will—Perfect in all ways. The end result of your Blind Faith will be the right outcome toward the salvation of your soul and a testimony for others to pursue GOD with Blind Faith.

The end is near for the bride on earth as she has known it. There is a new experience waiting her in MY Heavenlies. She will soar with ME and OUR love will be for eternity—a love that is everlasting. Place your heart in MY Hands. I am capable. You will be preserved from the evil coming.

I AM the GREAT HA MASHIACH.

Isaiah 40:31: But they that wait upon the LORD shall renew their strength; they shall mount up with wings as eagles; they shall run, and not be weary; and they shall walk, and not faint.

Wed, 15 Aug 2012

The LORD's Words: "I am about to shake free those who refuse to cling to ME."

Dear Faithful Followers of CHRIST:

"I don't worry about it—I am ready whenever HE comes."

Over and over when you try to warn Christians that the LORD is coming soon, for too many their pat answer is: "I don't worry about it, I am ready whenever HE comes."

Although many Christians feel that this is a good place to be—"ready whenever," with lukewarm interest in the topic, this is actually a very dangerous place to be. The LORD says that the only safe place for anyone is completely surrendered to GOD. Well if you are totally surrendered to GOD, then you would be in HIS Perfect Will. And, if you are, in fact, in GOD's Will you would therefore be AGGRESSIVELY WATCHING and LONGING for HIS Return. Your spirit should be on alert if you are in GOD's Perfect Will because this IS the true SPIRIT of GOD—a SPIRIT of eager watching, longing, looking forward to the LORD's Return. Remember the brief but powerful scripture in Luke 17:32: Remember Lot's wife? Too many are focused on this world for their answers, like Lot's wife and not turning to watch for (and pursue) the LORD.

GOD lays out the signs in the Bible to watch for and then says in Matthew 24:33-34: [33]So likewise ye, when ye shall see all these things, know that it is near, even at the doors. [34]Verily I say unto you, This generation shall not pass, till all these things be fulfilled. Now please note—all the scriptures that say to watch INTENTLY are not time sensitive as if there were a date to begin watching—but rather the scripture reads: for ye know not when the time is and thou shalt not know what hour I will come upon thee. But the scripture is extraordinarily clear there is a CROWN of RIGHTEOUSNESS FOR THOSE WHO LOVE HIS APPEARING and BLESSED IS HE THAT WATCHETH AND KEEPETH HIS GARMENTS. This IS the perfect Will of GOD to watch, to long, to have our garments ready—any other position of APATHY toward the return of our LORD is ABSOLUTELY OUT OF THE PERFECT WILL OF GOD. If your heart is not turning you to this direction and you aren't feeling a pull to be earnestly watching for the LORD—then you need to do a serious assessment of your spiritual position with GOD—you need to question if you are on the right path (the very narrow path that few find) or if you are following a way that is counter to the Will of GOD leading you to the very broad road...

2 Timothy 4:8: Henceforth there is laid up for me a crown of righteousness, which the LORD, the RIGHTEOUS JUDGE, shall give me at that day: and not to me only, but unto all them also that love HIS appearing.

Mark 13:33-37: [33]Take ye heed, watch and pray: for ye know not when the time is. [34]For the SON of Man is as a man taking a far journey, who left his house, and gave authority to his servants, and to every man his work, and commanded the porter to watch. [35]Watch ye therefore: for ye know not when the master of the house cometh, at even, or at midnight, or at the cockcrowing, or in the morning: [36]Lest coming suddenly he find you sleeping. [37]And what I say unto you I say unto all, Watch.

Revelation 3:3: Remember therefore how thou hast received and heard, and hold fast, and repent. If therefore thou shalt not watch, I will come on thee as a thief, and thou shalt not know what hour I will come upon thee.

Revelation 16:15: Behold, I come as a thief. Blessed is he that watcheth, and keepeth his garments, lest he walk naked, and they see his shame.

Matthew 7:14: Because strait is the gate, and narrow is the way, which leadeth unto life, and few there be that find it.

1 Peter 4:18: And if the righteous scarcely be saved, where shall the ungodly and the sinner appear?

There Is No Truth Found Anyplace But With Me

"It is an abomination to include ME among your earthly pursuits, as if I am just another lesser god."

(Words Received from Our LORD by Susan, August 9, 2012)

Susan, Yes I will give you Words:

The hour is approaching for MY Return. It comes nigh. MY children, I want you to begin focusing more intensely on your GOD as MY enemy creeps around looking for who he can snatch away, who he can hinder, who he can defile. He is wretched and will stop at nothing to provoke and bring harm to MY children, even those who are spoken for, chosen, and called for special work in the Kingdom—MY Kingdom on earth.

This is his delight to pull down MY children; to lead them away from Truth and Safety, MY Truth, MY Safety. You must stay vigilant in seeking ME, focus on ME, fixate on ME—do not look to the right or the left. There is only hopelessness when you move away from GOD back to the world.

O' yes, there are answers in the world, but all the wrong answers and lies misleading you from MY Will, MY Path, and MY Way to the road everlasting. Don't be deceived. There is no Truth found anyplace but with ME—where all Truth rests.

I hold the key to eternity. MY Blood is the covering that shields you from your deserved condemnation, that keeps you pure and holy before ME, so that you can stand before MY Presence—MY Holy Presence. Without it, you would be lost—found guilty, and punished for eternity.

This is very serious, MY children. Very few grasp the seriousness of this and how important it is to come to ME, surrender, repent, and make things right between US.

I want full surrender—nothing less will do. There are no answers for you anywhere else.

Children, there is great tribulation coming to the earth. Many do not believe this but it is true—don't be caught unawares. Many will be caught in the trap of MY enemy with no escape. This is what is coming to MY lukewarm children who choose not to watch for their LORD, who choose not to heed MY Warnings, and read MY Book.

These are MY children, who look for all the excuses to run from their GOD back into the arms of a dying, decaying world. Soon this world, disguised as a hopeful promising future, will be exposed as a dark, cruel ending for those who are left to face the worst. Don't be among them—run into MY Open, Saving Arms. There is only a short time remaining to receive clean garments, pure heart from the filling of MY SPIRIT and by seeking ME through intimacy.

You are selling yourself short if you think otherwise. I cannot be pleased with a casual relationship by hearts that are cool. This is MY dying and lost church of the lukewarm: those WHO believe they can be with the world and ME both. It is an abomination to include ME among your earthly pursuits, as if I am just another lesser god. If you handle the Holy and then place ME back upon your shelf, you will find yourself outside MY Kingdom when I come to rescue MY bride.

Proceed with caution. MY enemy seeks to destroy you. You are no match for him apart from MY Hand of protection, MY Armor to shield you. Only I can keep you safe from the trouble coming on the earth.

Turn and face ME. Give ME your hand. Let ME take you into MY Arms. Time is of the essence. Don't delay. Give ME your all so I can give you MY All. Exchange darkness for light. Let ME vanquish your fears and bring you to wholeness. The time is short: think wisely the use of your time. Fill it with your GOD.

I am the GOD WHO controls all time and space: I AM the LIGHT EVERLASTING!

1 Peter 5:8: Be sober, be vigilant; because your adversary the devil, as a roaring lion, walketh about, seeking whom he may devour:

Matthew 22:14: For many are called, but few are chosen.

Hebrews 9:12: Neither by the blood of goats and calves, but by HIS OWN Blood HE entered in once into the holy place, having obtained eternal redemption for us.

Matthew 24:21: For then shall be great tribulation, such as was not since the beginning of the world to this time, no, nor ever shall be.

Exodus 20:3: Thou shalt have no other gods before ME.

Ephesians 6:11: Put on the whole armour of GOD, that ye may be able to stand against the wiles of the devil.

Romans 13:12: The night is far spent, the day is at hand: let us therefore cast off the works of darkness, and let us put on the armour of light.

"I am about to shake free those who refuse to cling to ME."

(Words Received from Our LORD by Susan, August 10, 2012)

Daughter, listen as I give you Words:

Children of the MOST HIGH GOD, listen to ME, this is your FATHER Speaking: full of Love and Compassion…Eternal Love.

I am ready to remove MY bride—bring her home to the love, peace, and laughter that awaits her. Children, it is coming swiftly and only a few are paying attention: MY loyal bride, who is not seduced by this evil world. She is not caught up, mesmerized, by the world that MY rebellious children are turning to now instead of ME, their GOD. Futile: this is the world and its ways—what it offers MY children—a world of futility, but yet MY lost children cling—they pant after empty pursuits and base their lives on a future that is non-existent—one they have created in their own minds—one that is far from the reality of what lies shortly ahead.

They believe the world to be more of the same of what they already know, but the composition of the world is about to change dramatically and soon the world will not look the same and this world will be a far cry from the world that has existed. Even now, MY enemy is taking over all aspects of life as you have known it and altering the complexion of things to come shortly.

Your world is about to turn upside down, MY children. The only safe place is with your feet firmly planted on the ROCK—all other ground is sinking sand. Children, you know of what I Speak. Don't be asleep when I come for MY own. Awaken…be alert…focus on ME. No more sidetracks—just keep your eyes on ME. I am ready to deliver MY bride out to safety and no one can stop ME and MY Plans. I, GOD, will do as I say.

This world needs a spiritual shaking, but alas the shakeup will come for the left behind lukewarm church that will very soon be shaken to the core by the shock of what she will be left to face for her refusal to follow closely after ME, her GOD. This is the punishment coming for having a loose relationship with ME and not hanging on tightly. I am about to shake free those who refuse to cling to ME and would rather grip the world.

Soon those who hold onto the world too tightly will know the outcome of their choices as I leave them behind and take MY true church to safety. This is MY Plan and no one can stop ME from performing that which I have foretold.

Get ready MY church, MY chosen. The hour approaches for your rescue. I have said I will do it and MY Word is True. Make yourselves ready. Turn to ME. Wash your robes in MY Blood. Surrender and repent. I will do a big work in your life if you just lay it at MY Feet. This is MY Desire.

Come, Come! Now is the time! Children, the door will not remain open once I shut it. Choose for ME.

This is your LORD and SAVIOR

Luke 6:46-49: [46]And why call ye ME, LORD, LORD, and do not the things which I say? [47]Whosoever cometh to ME, and heareth my sayings, and doeth them, I will shew you to whom he is like: [48]He is like a man which built an house, and digged deep, and laid the foundation on a rock: and when the flood arose, the stream beat vehemently upon that house, and could not shake it: for it was founded upon a rock. [49]But he that heareth, and doeth not, is like a man that without a foundation built an house upon the earth; against which the stream did beat vehemently, and immediately it fell; and the ruin of that house was great.

Psalm 112:7: He shall not be afraid of evil tidings: his heart is fixed, trusting in the LORD.

Revelation 3:15-16: [15]I know thy works, that thou art neither cold nor hot: I would thou wert cold or hot. [16]So then because thou art lukewarm, and neither cold nor hot, I will spue thee out of MY Mouth.

Matthew 25:10: And while they went to buy, the bridegroom came; and they that were ready went in with him to the marriage: and the door was shut.

18. Don't Spend Another Moment Outside Of My Precious Will

The LORD's Words: These Words should ring in your ears: "I AM COMING!"

Words of the LORD:

"The people will soon be engulfed with so much evil they will not know where to turn for answers."

(Words Received from Our LORD by Susan, August 16, 2012)

Yes daughter, let US begin:

The tide is changing swiftly. The course of evil is moving. It is rushing. It is branching, growing, and flowing over the land like a river of death and destruction. The people will soon be engulfed with so much evil, they will not know where to turn for answers. I am the ONLY WAY to freedom, to peace, and life everlasting. I hold the keys to eternal life.

I am the ONE WHO Orchestrates salvation, WHO brings together the lost with life everlasting leading to the safe passage to GOD and eternal freedom—MY Blood Covering. There is no other way to be saved. MY Sacrifice on the cross is your free gift to free you from your sin chains, to unlock the things that bind you and hold you back from your salvation.

I am waiting by an open door—wide open. There is nothing to deter you from walking in—only the condition of your heart. You must place ME above all your other earthly pursuits. I can't tolerate second place. Not before: money…position…family…there can be NOTHING… that comes before ME in your heart.

I am a GOD WHO Requires first place positioning in your life. All who choose everything else above their GOD will be sorely disappointed when they find themselves in a kingdom that is bereft of GOD—a dark kingdom that is empty of love, peace, safety, well-being, and replaced with terror, torment, and punishment. This is what you trade for when you fill your life with worldly pursuits above the Will of GOD: if you think any different, then you are mistaken, misled, deceived by MY enemy. HE has deceived many and most are blinded from Truth and will be led away into eternal captivity by MY enemy. He delights in destroying MY children and bringing them to eternal hell. This is his mission to kill, steal, and destroy.

Don't let him pull you away from the Truth. Repent of your sins; come to ME in remorse and surrender. Lay it all before ME. Give ME your heart, soul, mind, and strength. Let ME fill you with MY HOLY SPIRIT and MY Light, Eternal Light.

You are wasting precious time. Don't spend another moment outside of MY Precious Will. It is MY Will for your life. No more guesswork about your future, no more anxiety about what will happen next. Let ME give you a future and a hope. I am the WAY, the TRUTH, and the LIFE.

MY Salvation is complete. Come bury your head on MY Shoulder. Let ME wipe away your tears and troubles. I am willing. I am MIGHTY to SAVE. Run into MY Open Arms. There isn't a moment to lose. The gate is open. The bar is up. Fly away with your LORD when I come for MY bride.

I am the GENTLE LAMB,

SAVIOR, HUSBAND, KING.

Revelation 3:18: I counsel thee to buy of ME gold tried in the fire, that thou mayest be rich; and white raiment, that thou mayest be clothed, and that the shame of thy nakedness do not appear; and anoint thine eyes with eyesalve, that thou mayest see.

Matthew 10:37: He that loveth father or mother more than ME is not worthy of ME: and he that loveth son or daughter more than ME is not worthy of ME.

Matthew 6:24: No man can serve two masters: for either he will hate the one, and love the other; or else he will hold to the one, and despise the other. Ye cannot serve GOD and mammon.

Mark 12:30: And thou shalt love the LORD thy GOD with all thy heart, and with all thy soul, and with all thy mind, and with all thy strength: this is the first commandment.

John 14:6: JESUS saith unto him, I am the WAY, the TRUTH, and the LIFE: no man cometh unto the FATHER, but by ME.

Revelation 21:4: And GOD shall wipe away all tears from their eyes; and there shall be no more death, neither sorrow, nor crying, neither shall there be any more pain: for the former things are passed away.

Revelation 22:17: And the SPIRIT and the bride say, Come. And let him that heareth say, Come. And let him that is athirst come. And whosoever will, let him take the water of life freely.

19. My Kingdom Will Consist Of Those ... Few Who Have Found Me To Be Worthy Of Their Utmost Devotion

These Words should ring in your ears: "I AM COMING!"

(Words Received from Our LORD by Susan, August 17, 2012)

Children, it is I, your LORD.

These Words should ring in your ears: "I AM COMING!"

Regardless of what those say around you, I am coming to take MY bride home to show her MY Beauty. She has waited patiently and MY Father has been patient, and soon I will unite with MY people, MY true worshippers, MY church, MY bride—those chosen to rule and reign in MY Kingdom for eternity. This is MY bride. Her key role is to serve her GOD in close proximity for all time. There is only love and a hopeful future for MY sweet bride.

MY Kingdom will consist of those I am placing closest to ME, the few who have found ME to be worthy of their utmost devotion. This is MY Kingdom, full of devoted followers—those who recognize that I am a Faithful GOD, True to MY Words, requiring first place position in the hearts of MY chosen few, those who pursue ME over all other earthly, temporal loves.

MY Love is worth pursuing. It is an ever-flowing fountain—everlasting love. MY Love cannot be stopped or slowed down. It is ever-increasing, growing, bountiful. This Love cannot be found in anyplace else, look though you may, it is vain wanderings leading to empty hands.

The world is a shallow, thin representation of love. Only MY Love sets the standard. Only MY Love is the source of all love found in the universe. Everything else is a copy of MY Eternal Love. Sad are those who settle for a weak, dying counterfeit in this world. You are settling for a weak facsimile of the Real Love of GOD—Love that cannot be copied and experienced like the authentic experience you have with the ONE, True GOD, JEHOVAH.

MY Love is a Mountain, a Holy Mountain. It is a stabilizing force of wholeness, peace, sound mind, perfect love—Faithful Love—Ultimate Love.

If you settle for the world, then you will soon be empty and lost, drifting for eternity outside MY Love, in hell: tormented and tortured.

You must decide—will you come into this Great Love—GOD's Love? I will not wait forever on MY children. Time is limited for this world. Don't find yourself outside of MY Love.

The ETERNAL LOVER of your soul.

Psalm 145:20: The LORD preserveth all them that love HIM: but all the wicked will HE destroy.

Proverbs 8:17: I love them that love ME; and those that seek ME early shall find ME.

Preparation Instructions to be the bride of CHRIST:

(Words Received from Our LORD by Susan, May 4, 2012)

Only I give the Power you need to keep you in MY Will. The flesh cannot succeed at staying in the Will of GOD. Only by MY Power is any man successful in walking in MY Will—flesh cannot accomplish this task. It is the Power of the HOLY SPIRIT.

A partial surrender does not allot the fullness of MY SPIRIT to bring the individual under the controlling Power of MY SPIRIT thus they cannot successfully ward off evil, sin, and be in MY Will. They are considered "lukewarm" and lost. Partial surrender is not "surrender." Make no mistake; a partial surrender leads to death the same as an outright denial of ME as GOD.

Repentance is "key" to the person's surrender. If they are still believing they have no sin or they don't need forgiveness how can they be freed by the evil that still controls them?

Remorse over sin is the beginning of healing—healing heart, soul, spirit—all is interrelated. A repentant heart, a humble heart, can receive the salvation of their soul and will enter MY Kingdom upon receiving the HOLY SPIRIT by baptism.

This is part of releasing the person into freedom to be freed of demonic spirits: true remorse over past sin, acknowledgement of sin before a HOLY GOD and then the filling of MY SPIRIT and total submission to MY Ways and to ME as the individual's LORD and MASTER.

All other expressions are weak and ineffectual. The person must be submitted to ME completely to be relieved of the power of MY enemy and I must be their undisputed MASTER so that the individual can be walking in MY Will conquering sin and filled with the Power of MY SPIRIT. Not before will the individual be able to deal successfully with vanquishing sin in their lives. This is the "narrow path." All other paths lead to destruction.

Deuteronomy 30:19: I call heaven and earth to record this day against you, that I have set before you life and death, blessing and cursing: therefore choose life that both thou and thy seed may live:

Your Lamp Oil Filled? The LORD will take only those 'sold out' to HIM and filled with the HOLY SPIRIT in the coming rapture of the church (remember, only the five virgins with full oil lamps are ready when the Bridegroom comes). If you don't think you are 'sold out' to HIM because you are caught up in things of this world then there is still time if you engage yourself right now in a relentless pursuit of knowing and following HIM. You must first be filled, 'baptized' with the HOLY SPIRIT.

You can be baptized in the HOLY SPIRIT right now: you can pray this suggested prayer: "In the LORD's Name, I pray to be baptized in the Names of the FATHER, the SON, and the HOLY SPIRIT. I pray to be filled up completely from the top of my head to the bottom of my toes. I pray for my Spiritual eyes to be opened and for the scales to fall off and I pray for a bolder testimony for the LORD JESUS and for MY OIL LAMP TO BE FILLED TO THE TOP. I surrender my ALL to the LORD and repent for all my sins from a sincere heart of remorse for these things done before a HOLY GOD." (You can also be prayed over by someone who has been baptized in the HOLY SPIRIT.)

You don't have to go anywhere or do anything as it has to do with the attitude of your heart. Just pray and you will receive through a sincere heart. Surrender your life over completely and repent from all your sins to the LORD. If you desire to be baptized in the HOLY SPIRIT, stop right now, where you are and pray. You can pray the suggested prayer above. You have ABSOLUTELY NOTHING TO LOSE AND EVERYTHING TO GAIN! When you pray to receive then 'press in' and read your bible or do it more and pray more.

Fasting also is recommended because it is by fasting from food, a meal, or something enjoyed such as your iPod, TV/movies, worldly pursuits, whatever we do that we 'die to our flesh.' Fasting does not replace salvation by JESUS' Blood at all. It just means we are dying to our flesh which is pleasing to the LORD for greater personal intimacy, seeking answers through prayers, whereas salvation is a free gift from GOD and not earned by any human act of sacrifice. These are verses that support a second baptism (the other being water baptism—the water baptism can come before or after the HOLY SPIRIT baptism) given from the HOLY SPIRIT:

Matthew 3:11: "As for me, I baptize you with water for repentance, but HE WHO is coming after me is mightier than I, and I am not fit to remove HIS sandals; HE will baptize you with the HOLY SPIRIT and fire."

Mark 1:8: "I baptized you with water; but HE will baptize you with the HOLY SPIRIT."

Luke 3:16: "John answered and said to them all, 'As for me, I baptize you with water; but ONE is coming WHO is mightier than I, and I am not fit to untie the thong of HIS sandals; HE will baptize you with the HOLY SPIRIT and fire."

John 1:33: "And I did not recognize HIM, but HE WHO sent me to baptize in water said to me, "HE upon WHOM you see the SPIRIT descending and remaining upon HIM, this is the ONE WHO baptizes in the HOLY SPIRIT."

Acts 1:5: "For John baptized with water, but you shall be baptized with the HOLY SPIRIT not many days from now."

Acts 11:15-16: " [15]And as I began to speak, the Holy Ghost fell on them, as on us at the beginning. And I remembered the Word of the LORD, how HE used to say, 'John baptized with water, but you shall be baptized with the HOLY SPIRIT.'"

Isaiah 52:14: as many were astonished at THEE; HIS visage was so marred more than any man and HIS form more than the sons of men.

Matthew 10:32: Whosoever therefore shall confess ME before men, him will I confess also before MY FATHER which is in heaven.

Romans 10:9: That if thou shalt confess with thy mouth the LORD JESUS, and shalt believe in thine heart that GOD hath raised HIM from the dead, thou shalt be saved.

Romans 10:10: For with the heart man believeth unto righteousness; and with the mouth confession is made unto salvation.

Matthew 7:22-23: [22] Many will say to me in that day, LORD, LORD, have we not prophesied in THY name? And in THY name have cast out devils? And in THY name done many wonderful works? [23] And then will I profess unto them, I never knew you: depart from me, ye that work iniquity. Okay wow—get this—these people were doing stuff you would expect church people to be doing—yet they were told to depart from the LORD—that doesn't sound like once saved, always saved…

1 Corinthians 9:27: But I keep under my body, and bring it into subjection: lest that by any means, when I have preached to others, I myself should be a castaway. This would appear that the Apostle Paul, who said this, was concerned over his eternal salvation and

surely Paul was once saved by the time he said this as he had preached to others...

Philippians 2:12: Wherefore, my beloved, as ye have always obeyed, not as in my presence only, but now much more in my absence, work out your own salvation with fear and trembling. If it is once saved, always saved—why all the fear and trembling to work out your own salvation?

1 Peter 4:18: And if the righteous scarcely be saved, where shall the ungodly and the sinner appear? No need to comment on this scripture...

Matthew 7:13-14: [13] Enter ye in at the strait gate: for wide is the gate, and broad is the way, that leadeth to destruction, and many there be which go in thereat: [14] Because strait is the gate, and narrow is the way, which leadeth unto life, and few there be that find it.—this doesn't sound like the masses who have been once saved always saved—sounds like a few finding salvation.

Hi Susan,

I want to share to you about a dream I had last night. Maybe you could help me to understand it. I don't know if it was a message or a confirmation. I was reading Angels on Assignment by Roland Buck before I went to sleep. Thanks and God bless!

The Dream, August 24, 2012:

I heard a Voice in my dream saying, "I will make YOUR enemies YOUR footstool!" Then, I saw the Temple Mount. I knew it was the Temple Mount, because I recognized its golden dome. Then, I saw a mushroom, than a mushroom cloud formed like a nuclear explosion. When I woke, I could still clearly remember the dream and the Voice. I looked up on the Internet exactly about the words that I heard in my dream. I was surprised to know that it was the Psalm of David and it was mentioned many times in the Bible. I've been thinking about what that dream could mean to me.

Glenda Baybay, Austria

Then I received this amazing interpretation from the LORD for Glenda's dream which I know is a very serious message the LORD wants put out:

August 25, 2012: Children this is your LORD Speaking. I will give this dream revelation. There is coming a revelation—the world is about to see the Hand of GOD Moving. I am about to shake the world. I am about to shake free my covenant people. How dare the hand of satan dare to touch MY people. I will bring lightning on high and shake lose the firm foundation of all the nations who come against MY chosen covenant people. Beware you evil doers: there is an hour coming of darkness, so dark that no one will be able to see past their own arm. This darkness is evil gathering on all four corners of the earth. Hark ye who will listen: for those who will listen I will give much—for those who turn away, I will take what little you hold onto. Let this serve as a warning to you, you evil doers and scoundrels around the world who come against MY covenant people.

Luke 20:41-43: [1]And HE said unto them, How say they that CHRIST is David's SON? [42]And David himself saith in the book of Psalms, The LORD said unto my LORD, Sit THOU on MY Right Hand, [43']Till I make THINE enemies THY footstool.

20. Stop Struggling, Looking For That Which Can Only Be Found In Me

Words of the LORD:

"Men may think they can alter the course of this growing evil, but it cannot be stopped by any human."

(Words Received from Our LORD by Susan, August 27, 2012)

Yes, Daughter Let US Begin:

There is a firestorm coming to the earth. It is growing. It is spreading. It is evil unchecked, unchallenged, unbridled. It is moving and growing. There will be no stopping it by any man. Men may think they can alter the course of this growing evil, but it cannot be stopped by any human.

Only I, GOD, will be able to bring this nightmare to a close. It will play out as the nations defiantly turn their back to ME, GOD…as they turn to block ME, GOD from all aspects of civilization, to eliminate ME from every part of life. I will release MY Protecting Hand over this sad earth and allow the havoc that is about to be wreaked over mankind.

Men everywhere reject ME—only a slight few…MY dear, humble bride…have made themselves ready and are watching for ME with enthusiasm. All other others have given themselves over to a lukewarm and cold position toward ME. MY bride denies herself—she comes to ME in whole-hearted surrender, leaving the wide path of the ways of the world. She seeks the finely defined narrow way that few find, few even seek.

She looks ardently for MY Way, MY Truth. She won't settle for second best from any other direction, only MY Perfect Will satisfies her soul—the longings of her soul. The world cannot satiate MY true bride—it only leaves her hungry, longing for more. The world only offers cold, empty promises. It is a cold attempt to lift the burden of a hungry soul. Only MY Truth, MY Will, MY Way truly fulfills the emptiness of a soul deprived of the SPIRIT of GOD. MY bride seeks until she finds the solution to her soul lost and empty without GOD.

Not even a partial filling satisfies the soul of MY pursuing bride because she knows there is no other place to find everlasting, unchanging fulfillment for the hungry, craving soul.

Are you MY bride? Do you hunger for wholeness of your mind and spirit? Is your soul restless, unquenched by a world that leaves you empty without purpose, without True Love? These things can only be found in ME, your LORD. I am the wholeness, peace, and serenity you seek, that your restless soul will never find in any other place or way. Search through many other worldly avenues: relationships, work, pursuit of wealth—only leaves you coming up dry and empty handed, feeling worthless and unloved.

You will not find love in these places—only MY Love fills the longings of the hungry heart and only MY Love will satisfy that lost, empty heart. Seek no more—I am here. I AM the ANSWER: the WAY, TRUTH, LIFE. Stop struggling, looking for that which can only be found in ME.

Children, too many are not hearing MY Words. They are not reading them and they refuse to listen and believe. This is not the hour to be sleeping. You are convinced the world has all the answers. She looks so self assured, so reliable. You will fall into the waiting arms of MY enemy. O' he waits patiently. He is in no hurry to see you fall, as long as he accomplishes his mission to bring you to the end he has planned for you. It matters not how long it takes to get you there. Be careful, because he will wait patiently if he believes he can trip you because of your traditions of men and your lack of knowledge. He will use these things to pull you away from Truth: a well-baited trap designed for your destruction.

His time is running out, so he is set on bringing down as many as possible. Even whole groups in churches that refuse to acknowledge the Power of the MY SPIRIT. If you are blocking the move of MY SPIRIT, you are blocking ME altogether! WE ARE ONE! Come to your senses. Time is running out!

There are only a few moments left to go. Seek ME. I am waiting for you children.

This is your LORD WHO Waits Patiently

Psalm 107:9: For HE satisfieth the longing soul, and filleth the hungry soul with goodness.

Psalm 63:1: O GOD, THOU art my GOD; early will I seek THEE: my soul thirsteth for THEE, my flesh longeth for THEE in a dry and thirsty land, where no water is;

Matthew 24:10-12: [10]And then shall many be offended, and shall betray one another, and shall hate one another. [11]And many false prophets shall rise, and shall deceive many. [12]And because iniquity shall abound, the love of many shall wax cold.

Matthew 24:9: Then shall they deliver you up to be afflicted, and shall kill you: and ye shall be hated of all nations for MY name's sake.

Matthew 7:14: Because strait is the gate, and narrow is the way, which leadeth unto life, and few there be that find it.

Matthew 15: Then came to JESUS scribes and Pharisees, which were of Jerusalem, saying, Why do THY disciples transgress the tradition of the elders? For they wash not their hands when they eat bread. But HE answered and said unto them, Why do ye also transgress the commandment of GOD by your tradition?

John 14:6: JESUS saith unto him, I am the WAY, the TRUTH, and the LIFE: no man cometh unto the FATHER, but by ME.

Hosea 4:6: MY people are destroyed for lack of knowledge: because thou hast rejected knowledge, I will also reject thee, that thou shalt be no priest to ME: seeing thou hast forgotten the law of thy GOD, I will also forget thy children.

Words of the LORD:

"What more passion can the world deliver to you than I can?"

(Words Received from Our LORD by Susan, August 28, 2012)

Yes daughter, Let US Begin:

MY children, who dwell upon the earth: there comes a day and an hour of MY Return. It is at hand, right around the corner. I have been brutally honest about what lies around the corner for those who refuse to prepare and be watching for MY descent to receive MY bride. There is great darkness that will soon cover the earth like a dark blanket of hopelessness, death, and destruction.

It will overwhelm those who remain to face it: those who refuse to watch for ME and to reconcile with ME through surrender and repentance. I ask nothing less than full surrender, repentance for all sins, forgiveness to all who have ever harmed you, and for a full oil lamp filling of MY SPIRIT. All must be complete, total—full. Partial surrender, partial forgiveness, partial repentance, and a half-full oil lamp will only keep you out of MY Kingdom.

You need to give all or give ME nothing at all—all or nothing. This is MY requirement for being ready to come with ME when I return to save MY own. I have no desire for your half-hearted commitment. It reeks and smells foul because you are still embracing the world when you give such a weak surrender.

You must believe that I, GOD, cannot be trusted or that the world appeals to you more than MY Great Love—MY Love as your SAVIOR—CREATOR—ETERNAL LOVER. What more can the world still give you that I, GOD—CREATOR cannot provide you? MY Love is complete, eternal, long-lasting, vibrant, and passionate!

I died a horrendous death: bruised and mutilated; surrounded and beaten with many blows. I was brought low, spit on, and torn apart by evil man. What more passion can the world deliver to you than I can?

MY Promises are True and the world I offer you will never disappoint. It is a beauty that cannot be understood or even comprehended by you now. This can all be yours if you would embrace MY Truth. Soon, very soon, MY Coming will come to pass and the hour approaches. So you can be ready or you can reject MY Plan and choose for the way to hell: the wide road. Many have gone before you, many will yet go. Don't be among them.

Now is the time to choose to be unique: the few, the focused—walking on the truly narrow way. I can lead you on this path but you must turn and follow. This is what I ask. What I require. Don't leave the path: so many leave it never to find it: Hold MY Hand. Let ME Guide you onto MY Path—I am the NARROW WAY. Only I lead to MY FATHER. Only MY Love and Power will save you. Come to know ME. I will not take second place seating in your heart. Consider this thoughtfully. Your eternal outcome depends on this choice.

If you want to be saved, come to ME NOW—I will listen. I will hear. I long to save you from destruction. I died to do it. Now let ME finish MY Work in your heart.

Come to ME Now. Minutes, only minutes to go.

Your LOVE and HEART'S RULER

Matthew 12:30: He that is not with ME is against ME; and he that gathereth not with ME scattereth abroad.

Revelation 3:16: So then because thou art lukewarm, and neither cold nor hot, I will spue thee out of MY Mouth.

Psalm 22:16: For dogs have compassed ME: the assembly of the wicked have enclosed ME: they pierced MY Hands and MY Feet.

Psalm 20:7: Some trust in chariots, and some in horses: but we will remember the Name of the LORD our GOD.

Hebrews 12:2: Looking unto JESUS the AUTHOR and FINISHER of our faith; WHO for the joy that was set before HIM endured the cross, despising the shame, and is set down at the Right Hand of the Throne of GOD.

Fri, 7 Sep 2012

The LORD's Words: "I want to talk to MY church...MY bride,"

The LORD's Words for Today (Posted at www.End-Times-Prophecy.Com)

A Letter to the Lukewarm Church:

Lukewarmers: you know who you are—you talk about being around for the next twenty years. You put up every argument against the idea of the LORD's soon return. Although the Bible is clear about the requirement of WATCHING for the LORD—you say watching isn't important—you are ready whenever... You have your own future all mapped out—who cares about inquiring for GOD's Will for your life? You are all caught up in how men can fix the economy, politics, and world problems apart from GOD. You love to misquote scripture to support your scoffing and nay-saying positions. Calling on GOD is only for those who are in a real bind—those who finally connect with GOD when a big crisis happens. Then when the crisis passes—you go back to focusing on the world and your love for it. You sure don't want GOD's Will for your life to get in the way of your own future plans.

Lukewarmers: you're in for a shock—your plans are about to sail out the window—as if they were solid anyway. You don't have twenty or thirty years to go and here's just ONE reason why: Go to any library, bookstore—flip through the cable channels or visit the current movies: EVIL abounds. Topics range from new age hocus pocus...occult obsession...mammon overload...repackaged, modernized paganism...pornography on steroids...and mega church environments with a form of godliness but denying the power thereof. Go down to any library anywhere and check out the books for the youth. This generation will not rebound from the evil it has escalated into. The total depravity reflected by the focus of the materials put before the youth today has NO foothold on future survival with its zero tolerance of GOD and the Bible. So apart from the guidance of the Bible, and the Power of the HOLY SPIRIT, what hope is there for this society to turn itself around? Who really wants to see what ten or twenty more years of a completely immoral culture will bring? Good thing we won't have to—that is if you are really looking for the LORD's Return but if your plan is to run with the pack it is not going to serve you very well because the road is narrow and few find it.

Galatians 5:19-21: [19]Now the works of the flesh are manifest, which are these; Adultery, fornication, uncleanness, lasciviousness, [20]Idolatry, witchcraft, hatred, variance, emulations, wrath, strife, seditions, heresies, [21]Envyings, murders, drunkenness, revellings, and such like: of the which I tell you before, as I have also told you in time past, that they which do such things shall not inherit the Kingdom of GOD.

Matthew 24:12: And because iniquity shall abound, the love of many shall wax cold.

2 Timothy 3:1-5: This know also, that in the last days perilous times shall come. [2]For men shall be lovers of their own selves, covetous, boasters, proud, blasphemers, disobedient to parents, unthankful, unholy, [3]Without natural affection, trucebreakers, false accusers, incontinent, fierce, despisers of those that are good, [4]Traitors, heady, high-minded, lovers of pleasures more than lovers of GOD; [5]Having a form of godliness, but denying the power thereof: from such turn away.

James 4:13-14: [13]Go to now, ye that say, Today or tomorrow we will go into such a city, and continue there a year, and buy and sell, and get gain: [14]Whereas ye know not what shall be on the morrow. For what is your life? It is even a vapour that appeareth for a little time, and then vanisheth away.

Isaiah 31:1: Woe to them that go down to Egypt for help; and stay on horses, and trust in chariots, because they are many; and in horsemen, because they are very strong; but they look not unto the HOLY ONE of Israel, neither seek the LORD!

James 4:4: Ye adulterers and adulteresses, know ye not that the friendship of the world is enmity with GOD? Whosoever therefore will be a friend of the world is the enemy of GOD.

2 Peter 3:3-4: [3]Knowing this first, that there shall come in the last days scoffers, walking after their own lusts, [4]and saying, Where is the promise of HIS coming? For since the fathers fell asleep, all things continue as they were from the beginning of the creation.

Revelation 3:16: So then because thou art lukewarm, and neither cold nor hot, I will spue thee out of MY Mouth.

What I Said So Long Ago Would Happen Is Happening

"They do not want to face what is coming, so they have locked themselves up away from the Truth."

(Words Received from Our LORD by Susan, September 2, 2012)

So daughter, WE can begin:

Children, this is your GOD. I am a GOD WHO is Truthful. What I say…goes. I have the key that unlocks the future. What I said so long ago would happen is happening. Those who know, see it— those who refuse to look cannot see and they are paralyzed by the Truth.

The Truth has them in a headlock. They do not want to face what is coming, so they have locked themselves up away from the Truth: be it their pursuit of the world in a myriad of ways so that they do not have to see what is happening before their very eyes. They believe if they don't see it, they don't have to face it and then what is True seems to be only rumors, but reality is about to sink in…

For those who live to find Truth and to be in MY Will they will find safety and long life. For those who reject MY Truth through MY Word—Signs—and MY messengers, these will know destruction and heartache and grief. I am so very clear in MY Writings—those of the past and those through MY messengers today. MY Truth always lines up MY Words with what comes into being.

Children, there comes a time when I will be ready to bring out MY church to safety, because the world will be so grim, so ugly, so desolate and foreboding. I will not allow MY church to endure much more. She is about to be removed to safe keeping…to her eternal abode…a residence near her GOD. The world is growing dark around her and she is precious to ME. I will not stand for her rejection by others, who refuse to see the Truth, much longer.

So children, the hour approaches quickly. You will know what to watch for as MY Signs are all clearly outlined throughout MY Book. The raptured church is about to be brought out of the way, then those left will contend with MY Wrath.

Buckle down and pay attention. Make your way to ME. Repent of your sin life and forgive all those around you. Surrender fully and let ME recline your spirit to take it into a safe place. This all lies straight ahead.

Never lose heart. Turn and face GOD. Give ME your full affection—nothing else will do. I give you MY All. I ask for your all.

This is your LORD and SAVIOR

ABOVE ALL ELSE, SEEK MY FACE

Deuteronomy 32:4: HE is the ROCK, HIS work is perfect: for all HIS ways are judgment: a GOD of Truth and without iniquity, just and right is HE.

Isaiah 55:11: So shall MY Word be that goeth forth out of MY Mouth: it shall not return unto ME void, but it shall accomplish that which I please, and it shall prosper in the thing whereto I sent it.

Joel 2:28: And it shall come to pass afterward, that I will pour out MY SPIRIT upon all flesh; and your sons and your daughters shall prophesy, your old men shall dream dreams, your young men shall see visions:

Revelation 3:19: As many as I love, I rebuke and chasten: be zealous therefore, and repent.

Mark 11:25-26: [25]And when ye stand praying, forgive, if ye have ought against any: that your FATHER also which is in heaven may forgive you your trespasses. [26]But if ye do not forgive, neither will your FATHER which is in heaven forgive your trespasses.

Mark 12:30: And thou shalt love the LORD thy GOD with all thy heart, and with all thy soul, and with all thy mind, and with all thy strength: this is the first commandment.

21. I Am Looking Forward To Meeting With You

Words of the LORD:

"I want to talk to MY church...MY bride,"

(Words Received from Our LORD by Susan, September 4, 2012)

Daughter, listen to MY Words:

I want to talk to MY church...MY bride, now:

Dear Church,

I am your GOD. I am a very Happy GOD. I am looking forward to meeting with you. I will be stationed at the gate to pick you up. The hour is coming. Yes and the train is on time. Soon you will be boarding. I have a special coach waiting for you. It is marked "Bride's Coach." It is for those who are at the gate waiting patiently, ready and waiting, watching and anxious—anticipating the GROOM! I am ready for you bride. There is beauty on high—the mountain top. It is MY Heart!

Are you ready? Do you even know I am coming?

The world is growing into a heavy, thick darkness spreading and covering all mankind. MY bride shines out past the dark covering. She is like beams of light—lighting the way to MY Truth. All else is darkness, false words: words not given by GOD to mislead the people.

Any time you hear words contrary to what MY Word lays out, stay far away from it—doctrines of devils. Much falseness abounds. The world seeks truth, but through words it most wants to hear, not from MY Word or from MY Mouth.

This is the great hour of discernment. It is time to be discerning O' church. Stop listening to every word that goes out without seeking ME for confirmation through MY SPIRIT, MY Word. Not all words are Truthful. There is much deception flying around to confuse MY bride, to lead her astray, to pull her off the narrow path. I tell you children, devils lurk about to muddy the waters with untruths and to polarize MY people, to lead them astray, and to throw them off MY Truth away from the straight path.

Pray for discernment, pray for Truth, pray to receive the Words straight from the Mouth of GOD and not from alternate routes: made up truths and lies from evil sources. All is not as it seems. MY adversary comes as an angel of light looking for who he can deceive and mislead. Test the waters by the Power of MY SPIRIT. Only HE can lead you to all Truth—no other—not by the interpretations of men, but by MY SPIRIT providing confirmations through MY SPIRIT's Leading and Direction.

Submit yourself to ME wholly by full surrender, repent and forgive those around you. Only by full submission can MY SPIRIT function fully in your heart leading you to all Truth. These times are dangerous MY children—even treacherous. Don't be deceived by devils and lies from the enemy. Be on guard. Submit wholly to your GOD for assurance of the Truth.

I am coming! Words to the contrary are lies. Get ready MY church, MY bride. Your BRIDEGROOM COMETH! Look up, your redemption draweth nigh.

Micah 4:1: But in the last days it shall come to pass, that the mountain of the house of the LORD shall be established in the top of the mountains, and it shall be exalted above the hills; and people shall flow unto it.

Isaiah 2:2: And it shall come to pass in the last days, that the mountain of the LORD's house shall be established in the top of the mountains, and shall be exalted above the hills; and all nations shall flow unto it.

Ephesians 5:8: For ye were sometimes darkness, but now are ye Light in the LORD: walk as children of Light:

2 Corinthians 11:14: And no marvel; for satan himself is transformed into an angel of light.

Colossians 1:13: WHO hath delivered us from the power of darkness, and hath translated us into the kingdom of HIS Dear SON:

2 Timothy 1:13-14: [13]Hold fast the form of sound words, which thou hast heard of me, in faith and love which is in CHRIST JESUS. [14]That good thing which was committed unto thee keep by the HOLY GHOST which dwelleth in us.

1 Corinthians 2:10-14: [10]But GOD hath revealed them unto us by HIS SPIRIT: for the SPIRIT searcheth all things, yea, the deep things of GOD. [11]For what man knoweth the things of a man, save the spirit of man which is in him? Even so the things of GOD knoweth no man, but the SPIRIT of GOD. [12]Now we have received, not the spirit of the world, but the SPIRIT which is of GOD; that we might know the things that are freely given to us of GOD. [13]Which things also we speak, not in the words which man's wisdom

teacheth, but which the HOLY GHOST teacheth; comparing SPIRITUAL things with SPIRITUAL. [14]But the natural man receiveth not the things of the SPIRIT of GOD: for they are foolishness unto him: neither can he know them, because they are SPIRITUALLY discerned.

Tue, 11 Sep 2012

The LORD's Words: "I am not a GOD WHO can be mocked and men have mocked ME enough."

The LORD's Words for Today (Posted at www.End-Times-Prophecy.Com)

Dear Lukewarm Christians:

Why am I picking on you so much, lukewarm Christians? Because you are LOST and you don't even know it...

Revelation 3:16: So then because thou art lukewarm, and neither cold nor hot, I will spue thee out of my mouth.

Here is the solution to reverse the lukewarm condition:

Surrender your ALL to the LORD—your life—mind—soul—spirit—future plans—Give it all to the LORD—ask to be filled with the HOLY SPIRIT and to have a FULL OIL LAMP—(meaning: you give the HOLY SPIRIT all of you and you die to self to give complete control of your life over to the HOLY SPIRIT—back away from your pursuit/love of the world by the power of the HOLY SPIRIT.)

Here are some of the troubling symptoms of the lukewarm condition:

2 Timothy 3:5: Having a form of godliness, but denying the power thereof: from such turn away.

Without the Baptism or full oil lamp (not a half full oil lamp) filling of the HOLY SPIRIT you will have a form of godliness (religion) but deny the power of the HOLY SPIRIT—always doing things in the flesh apart from the HOLY SPIRIT—and you lose the benefit of greater understanding of the Bible, a bolder testimony, and the ability to conquer sin in your life by the power of the HOLY SPIRIT, instead you try to do it through the flesh which is impossible.

Now the lukewarm church wants to chase out the manifestations of the HOLY SPIRIT Filling which can be (based on the HOLY SPIRIT's choosing to whom HE will give what to): speaking in tongues; interpretations of tongues; visions/dreams; prophesy; Spiritual discernment—etc. Here is why the lukewarm church wants to contain it or eliminate it altogether: the religious spirit abounds in the lukewarm churches—a spirit of rebellion that operates right inside the church to put a stop to the essential and precious move of the HOLY SPIRIT—WHO alone enables the people to operate in the power of the SPIRIT and to be out of their prior lukewarm condition and ultimately saved. Here is more information on the religious spirit:

http://www.takehisheart.com/religiousspiritpythonsatan.htm

Also the lukewarm without the HOLY SPIRIT are not getting the benefit of correct understanding of the scripture. Understanding the scripture comes by the leading of the HOLY SPIRIT exclusively and not by the leadings, teachings of men: 1 Corinthians 2:10-14: [10] But GOD hath revealed them unto us by HIS SPIRIT: for the SPIRIT searcheth all things, yea, the deep things of GOD. [11] For what man knoweth the things of a man, save the spirit of man which is in him?

Even so the things of GOD knoweth no man, but the SPIRIT of GOD. [12] Now we have received, not the spirit of the world, but the SPIRIT which is of GOD; that we might know the things that are freely given to us of GOD. [13] Which things also we speak, not in the words which man's wisdom teacheth, but which the HOLY GHOST teacheth; comparing spiritual things with spiritual. [14] But the natural man receiveth not the things of the SPIRIT of GOD: for they are foolishness unto him: neither can he know them, because they are spiritually discerned.

http://www.takehisheart.com/holyspiritspiritualthings.htm

Now the lukewarm church is still caught up in the blending of the world with their faith—but the two cannot mix:

James 4:4: Ye adulterers and adulteresses, know ye not that the friendship of the world is enmity with GOD? Whosoever therefore will be a friend of the world is the enemy of GOD.

Matthew 7:22-23: [22] Many will say to ME in that day, LORD, LORD, have we not prophesied in THY Name? And in THY Name have cast out devils? And in THY Name done many wonderful works? [23] And then will I profess unto them, I never knew you: depart from ME, ye that work iniquity.

So the lukewarm church falls into trouble in two ways here: 1) she handles the things of GOD: going to church a couple days a week and praying every now and then—but not really pursuing GOD intimately and seeking the full surrender leading to a full oil lamp. So the lukewarm church never really experiences the powerful walk available through the fullness of the HOLY SPIRIT. And 2) the punishment will be much greater for the lukewarm church in hell—those who had access to the things of GOD but because of their casual relationship with HIM they pull back to pursue the world for answers and gratification that they should have instead found directly through GOD.

Proverbs 26:11: As a dog returneth to his vomit, so a fool returneth to his folly.

Hebrews 6:4-8: ⁴ For it is impossible for those who were once enlightened, and have tasted of the heavenly gift, and were made partakers of the HOLY GHOST, ⁵ And have tasted the good Word of GOD, and the powers of the world to come, ⁶ If they shall fall away, to renew them again unto repentance; seeing they crucify to themselves the SON of GOD afresh, and put HIM to an open shame. ⁷ For the earth which drinketh in the rain that cometh oft upon it, and bringeth forth herbs meet for them by whom it is dressed, receiveth blessing from GOD: ⁸ But that which beareth thorns and briers is rejected, and is nigh unto cursing; whose end is to be burned.

If you see yourself in this condition—lukewarm—you better RUN, not walk to seek the Baptism of the HOLY SPIRIT, to receive a full oil lamp through repentance of your sins and lukewarm condition, and to give a full surrender of your life and to be completely submitted to CHRIST (see the article within this letter below with more about the HOLY SPIRIT Baptism).

22. I Will Not Allow This World To Carry On Much Longer

"No man can stop the rage of MY Wrath that is coming over the earth."

(Words Received from Our LORD by Susan, September 9, 2012)

Yes, daughter, WE can begin:

Children this is your LORD Speaking:

Soon MY children, soon, the hour is coming. There is a great countdown. The world surrounds MY covenant people. They are being surrounded on all sides. The dogs surround her. They are ready to launch their attack. MY people feel isolated and abandoned by the world.

The world is an enmity to ME. It is all evil—filled with evil men, men whose hearts wax cold. The world embraces MY enemy as if evil is the answer to all their woes. They are jumping over the brink of destruction heading for disaster by holding tight to their evil intensions.

I will not allow this world to carry on much longer. Soon, I will remove MY bride and turn away, turn MY back to her. I will not be moved with sadness for the calamity coming her way. MY Heart will not pound with anticipation over the great darkness that will consumer her after I lift MY people out to safety. I will turn MY Face away from the evil that rules the land after MY bride is safely put away.

The people left on earth are about to swallow the cup of MY Wrath and to drink down the anger I have been burdened by from the overwhelming evil, rebellion, and rejection that the world has embraced. This rejection of GOD will not be tolerated much further. MY Patience has been tested and tried over and over again. But the limit of even MY Great Patience has been met and now the wrath of MY internal fire has been stoked and will pour out over the earth and it cannot be stopped. No man can stop the rage of MY Wrath that is coming over the earth.

The smoke of MY Fury will not be put out until I come back to settle the matter at MY Second Coming when I take control of evil man and MY enemy and take control over the earth again. MY anger has been aroused and I will deliver the justice that calls for MY burning retribution for those rebellious children who know ME not—who whole-heartedly reject MY truth, MY ways, MY Rule.

It is coming children. You hold life in your hands. Do you decide to stay and see how bad things will be or will you come out when I call up MY church to safety?

Come up to safety. Don't choose against ME. Don't choose death and destruction. Be wise. Read MY Word. Study it. Don't let lack of knowledge separate you from MY Truth, Salvation, and Escape from MY Wrath. You do not want to experience the force of MY Powerful Blows coming to this land of rebellion.

I am ready to unleash MY pent up fury and to show MYSELF Strong and True to MY Words. Prepare yourselves. Are you coming at the sound of the trumpet or are you ready to drink deep from the cup of MY Wrath? You choose. Now is the time.

Your GOD, Your CREATOR Has Spoken.

Psalm 22:16: For dogs have compassed ME: the assembly of the wicked have enclosed ME: they pierced MY Hands and MY Feet.

James 4:4: Ye adulterers and adulteresses, know ye not that the friendship of the world is enmity with GOD? Whosoever therefore will be a friend of the world is the enemy of GOD.

Matthew 24:12: And because iniquity shall abound, the love of many shall wax cold.

Obadiah 1:13:Thou shouldest not have entered into the gate of MY people in the day of their calamity; yea, thou shouldest not have looked on their affliction in the day of their calamity, nor have laid hands on their substance in the day of their calamity;

Hosea 4:6: MY people are destroyed for lack of knowledge: because thou hast rejected knowledge, I will also reject thee, that thou shalt be no priest to me: seeing thou hast forgotten the law of thy GOD, I will also forget thy children.

Deuteronomy 32:41: If I whet MY glittering sword, and MINE Hand take hold on judgment; I will render vengeance to MINE enemies, and will reward them that hate ME.

Zechariah 12:2: Behold, I will make Jerusalem a cup of trembling unto all the people round about, when they shall be in the siege both against Judah and against Jerusalem.

Nahum 1:2: GOD is JEALOUS, and the LORD revengeth; the LORD revengeth, and is furious; the LORD will take vengeance on his adversaries, and HE reserveth wrath for HIS enemies.

Luke 21:22: For these be the days of vengeance, that all things which are written may be fulfilled.

23. Repent Of Your Evil: Your Wicked Plans Of Making Goals And A Future Apart From Your God

"I am not a GOD WHO can be mocked and men have mocked ME enough."

(Words Received from Our LORD by Susan, September 10, 2012)

Let US Begin:

Children, this is the MOST HIGH. I am about to show MYSELF GREAT. I am about to show MYSELF TRUTHFUL. I am about to be the GREAT PROMISE KEEPER. I am a GOD WHO can be Trusted. What I say, goes!

Men try to rewrite history and the future outside of MY Word, MY Truth. They can try, but they won't succeed. I am not a GOD WHO can be mocked and men have mocked ME enough. I cannot be pushed by evil men as if I am just a man—flesh and blood man.

I am GOD—YAHWEH—EVERLASTING KING of kings, LORD of lords!

Soon, MY Wrath will pour out over the earth and there will be no stopping it by any flesh, human. This hour cannot be stopped. It is coming to pass as I instructed it would though evil man scoffs and clings to his dwindling future plans he devises through his own wicked heart apart from consulting his MAKER—CREATOR.

All is evil: to plan without consulting the Will of GOD. Soon these seeming sure plans will all pass away like dust on the wind—blowing like a great dust storm. All evil man's plans for a great non-existent future will come undone and be replaced by the realization that great evil has moved in and taken over. Any hope of the future men now devise in their wicked minds will soon run away like dissolving water colors.

Evil: this is the heart of men who do not acknowledge the will of GOD—self centered…prideful…self-serving men who seek ME not for their future plans. All is evil. Only MY Plans matter and count in the end. Do men not see this? The broad road to hell is paved with good intentions and great plans in the minds of men who never once inquire of their GOD how to live their lives as they should…by MY Book…MY Word…MY Will. These men bypass GOD and head straight to hell without ever once seeking MY Face. Repenting of their sin, and surrendering their all to ME: these are the ones who find the narrow path and make it into MY Eternal Kingdom—all others are lost in the broad kingdom of hell where there is outer darkness and eternal punishment.

"Harsh Words," you say…True Words, Saving Words for those who embrace them and choose to live by them. Face ME on your knees, repent of your evil: your wicked plans of making goals and a future apart from your GOD. I will bring you into right standing with ME and set you on the straight and narrow path.

Your time is short to come clean and make ready. Mockers and blasphemers of GOD will have no place in MY Kingdom.

I am a Great GOD of Patience and Kindness.

But, I Rule with an Iron Rod and I will not be tempted.

Try ME no more!

Psalm 107:11-12: [11]Because they rebelled against the Words of GOD, and condemned the counsel of the MOST HIGH: [12] Therefore

HE brought down their heart with labour; they fell down, and there was none to help.

Psalm 10:4: The wicked, through the pride of his countenance, will not seek after GOD: GOD is not in all his thoughts.

Proverbs 14:12: There is a way which seemeth right unto a man, but the end thereof are the ways of death.

Proverbs 16:2: All the ways of a man are clean in his own eyes; but the LORD weigheth the spirits.

Proverbs 16:25: There is a way that seemeth right unto a man, but the end thereof are the ways of death.

Ecclesiastes 12:14: For GOD shall bring every work into judgment, with every secret thing, whether it be good, or whether it be evil.

Ezekiel 14:12-20: [12] The Word of the LORD came again to me, saying,[13] Son of man, when the land sinneth against ME by trespassing grievously, then will I stretch out MINE Hand upon it, and will break the staff of the bread thereof, and will send famine upon it, and will cut off man and beast from it:[14] Though these three men, Noah, Daniel, and Job, were in it, they should deliver but their own souls by their righteousness, saith the LORD GOD.[15] If I cause noisome beasts to pass through the land, and they spoil it, so that it be desolate, that no man may pass through because of the beasts: [16] Though these three men were in it, as I live, saith the LORD GOD, they shall deliver neither sons nor daughters; they only shall be delivered, but the land shall be desolate. [17] Or if I bring a sword upon that land, and say, Sword, go through the land; so that I cut off man and beast from it: [18] Though these three men were in it, as I live, saith the LORD GOD, they shall deliver neither sons nor daughters, but they only shall be delivered themselves. [19] Or if I send a pestilence into that land, and pour out my fury upon it in blood, to cut off from it man and beast: [20] Though Noah, Daniel, and Job were in it, as I live, saith the LORD GOD, they shall deliver neither son nor daughter; they shall but deliver their own souls by their righteousness.

Psalm 2:9: THOU shalt break them with a rod of iron; THOU shalt dash them in pieces like a potter's vessel.

Revelation 2:27: And HE shall rule them with a rod of iron; as the vessels of a potter shall they be broken to shivers: even as I received of MY FATHER.

Revelation 19:15: And out of HIS Mouth goeth a sharp sword, that with it HE should smite the nations: and HE shall rule them with a rod of iron: and HE treadeth the winepress of the fierceness and wrath of ALMIGHTY GOD.

The LORD wanted me to include these Words received by my good friend Donna who also hears from HIM with this very serious warning:

Oh, Lord, people are not getting the soon sudden destruction and rapture message. Do you have words regarding this message?

Yes, my daughter, I have words. The people do not get it because they have their heads in the sand. They don't want to take their heads out because then they would have to look around and see that things aren't right in the world and they are never going to be because there is an antichrist system being set in place. Everything is there, it is just waiting to happen.

The people believe they are going to get Obama out of office and put Romney in. Do you have words regarding this line of thinking?

The people have always put their faith and trust in what they see and in what they believe they can do. This is no different. They believe they are going to get Obama out and put Romney in and all will be okay but this is not true. Obama will have a higher trump card than Romney. Whatever hand Romney plays Obama, by hook or crook, will come up with a higher point hand and win the game. This will cause destruction and death in the land.

What about the rapture, Lord? I know we can't know the day or time. What do you have to say?

The rapture is right around the corner. The people have been warned and better be ready. So few are ready, though. They shun the message and fight it because they don't want to change their lifestyle to accommodate for the rapture.

What is going to happen when the Bride is removed from the earth in the rapture?

There will be sudden destruction, a nuclear event, a solicited one will occur in the U.S. at the time of the rapture. This is what will elicit the rapture. I will not allow my Bride to be radiated or destroyed. She is Mine. I paid a high price on the cross for her and laid down my life for her. I will not allow evil men and an evil system to harm her in any way.

What will this mean for those left behind?

Those left behind will be the sorriest people on this earth. There will be great moans and groans and weeping sweeping across the earth. The earth will be in ruins because of multiple nuclear reactions across the globe, not only in the U.S. but all across the globe. The people will realize something very evil has happened. Marshall Law will be ushered in quickly to control the people because of widespread looting, robbery, and crime. People will be attacked and robbed on the streets, in their yards and in their homes. No one will be safe. There will be widespread hunger and lack of drinking water. People will become desperate and like wild animals. The world has never seen the evil that will be unleashed when the Bride is taken.

Is there a way for those left behind to be saved?

Yes, they must profess their faith in Me to authorities and refuse the RFID health care chip in their hand or forehead. They will then be arrested, tortured in FEMA camps and beheaded. These children will arrive in heaven in glory for they refused the mark of the beast, the health care chip. I will give them each a crown with jewels for their martyrdom.

Verses I am including to go with the Lord's words:

1 Thes. 5:1-3 NKJV 'But concerning the times and the seasons, brethren, you have no need that I should write to you. For you yourselves know perfectly that the day of the Lord so comes as a thief in the night. For when they say, "Peace and safety!" then sudden destruction comes upon them, as labor pains upon a pregnant woman. And they shall not escape.'

Prov. 28:26 NIV "Those who trust in themselves are fools, but those who walk in wisdom are kept safe."

Mark 13:32-33 NIV "No one knows about that day or hour, not even the angels in heaven, nor the Son, but only the Father. Be on guard! Be alert! You do not know when that time will come.

Revelation 20:4 NIV "I saw thrones on which were seated those who had been given authority to judge. And I saw the souls of those who had been beheaded because of their testimony about Jesus and because of the word of God. They had not worshiped the beast or its image and had not received its mark on their foreheads or their hands.

Donna McDonald 9/2/12

Now, I want to give you the Words I (Susan) received myself from the LORD about a year and a half to two years ago—I was in my living room at the time and completely without any warning the LORD Spoke these words to me: The people think they are going to get this man out of office (our president) and then things will go back to normal—NOT SO!—the problem goes much deeper than this—it is that the people have sunk to the level that they could have had this man over them in the first place.

Date: Sat, 15 Sep 2012

The LORD's Words: "You are fighting a brick wall if you carry on in th e belief I do not exist."

The LORD's Words for Today (Posted at www.End-Times-Prophecy.Com)

Dear Faithful Followers of CHRIST:

There is a shift that the Christians are facing up to in the world. But so many do not want to face what is happening. They do not want to see that the world and men are running out of options—answers. People are grasping at straws now. They are trying to convince themselves, that the lesser of two evils equals a righteous answer. Christians are using every kind of twisted explanations to accept the answers put forth by the secular world for their lives. Here is the shift—GOD is saying that men no longer offer good choices because they have all turned their hearts away from GOD. But Christians want to cling to the world and are trying to talk themselves into it with all sorts of arguments. GOD is doing a new thing. HE is showing the Christians now that the choice is between the world and CHRIST. Although the world has always been an enmity to GOD—the FATHER is saying: stop worrying about seeking ways to feel good about the answers men are giving to choose from—HE is saying look up your redemption draweth nigh for those who are watching.

You Have Dirt On Your Hands And You Can't Even See It

Words of the LORD:

"You are fighting a brick wall if you carry on in the belief I do not exist."

(Words Received from Our LORD by Susan, September 13, 2012)

Listen carefully as I give you Words:

Children, your LORD Speaks:

I am a TOWERING INFERNO of Love about to break forth over the world—I come bringing love…healing…wholeness of heart. I carry with ME salvation, a bright future. I am the ROCK—solid—strong—providing divine retribution to MY enemy. Soon the people will see that I am the SALVATION of the Nations, the MASTER with the Healing Touch.

There will be two peoples on earth at the time of MY Coming: The happiest of all peoples: MY bride and the sorriest of all people: those left to face MY enemy, those who rejected MY Words and rebelled against Ways, MY Will, MY Saving Grace. This is the destiny of the masses: few to salvation of their souls and most to face the horrors of the kingdom of hell come to earth—the reign and rule of MY enemy over MY rebellious children.

MY children who rebel:

You rebel against ME in many ways: you refuse to read MY Word and spend time in MY Truth. You grieve MY SPIRIT and deny the power of MY SPIRIT in your life because you prefer to work things out with your flesh against MY Will. You reach for the things of the world handling the unholy and then grasping for the holy as if the two can mingle so easily. This is an abomination to ME.

I find this putrid and I will spit you out for your double-minded ways. You are no better than LOT's Wife whoring after a world of death and decay. Surely you see you are unfit to come into MY Kingdom? You have dirt on your hands and you can't even see it. I will put you outside MY Kingdom where there is weeping and gnashing of teeth. That is the way of this adulterous generation: full of a form of godliness but denying the power thereof.

I am clear in MY Word. Come away from this blaspheming world—it is almost time for ME to choose who is coming out with ME to glory and who I have chose for destruction. The disposition of your heart determines MY choosing. Is your heart turned toward ME in rapid pursuit or is it pulling away to MY enemy toward outer darkness?

I know all, I see all. I know the inner most thoughts of a man. Nothing gets by ME. I know the thoughts, the actions, the deeds. Get right with your GOD NOW. This is the hour; tomorrow may be too late. You do not know what the next hour holds for your life. Why do you treat this decision with such contempt? Why do you think you have ultimate ownership of your soul and that I, GOD cannot be angered by your choosing against ME?

You are fighting a brick wall if you carry on in the belief I do not exist. You WILL come to know ME—how will WE meet: in waves of love or torrents of destruction and punishment? This is your part: choose for ME and I will raise you up to share eternity with ME. Come to terms with this choice. All men will be without excuse when they face ME. I will not hear excuses because there will be none. Now you must choose.

Bride stand ready,

Your LOVER Awaits.

Isaiah 52:10: The LORD hath made bare HIS Holy Arm in the eyes of all the nations; and all the ends of the earth shall see the Salvation of our GOD.

Proverbs 17:11: An evil man seeketh only rebellion: therefore a cruel messenger shall be sent against him.

Matthew 7:14: Because strait is the gate, and narrow is the way, which leadeth unto life, and few there be that find it.

James 1:8: A double minded man is unstable in all his ways.

Luke 17:32: Remember Lot's wife.

Matthew 22:8-14: [8] Then saith he to his servants, The wedding is ready, but they which were bidden were not worthy. [9] Go ye therefore into the highways, and as many as ye shall find, bid to the marriage. [10] So those servants went out into the highways, and gathered together all as many as they found, both bad and good: and the wedding was furnished with guests. [11] And when the king came in to see the guests, he saw there a man which had not on a wedding garment: [12] And he saith unto him, Friend, how camest thou in hither not having a wedding garment? And he was speechless. [13] Then said the king to the servants, Bind him hand and foot, and take him away, and cast him into outer darkness, there shall be weeping and gnashing of teeth. [14] For many are called, but few are chosen.

Luke 13:23-28: [23] Then said one unto him, LORD, are there few that be saved? And he said unto them, [24] Strive to enter in at the strait gate: for many, I say unto you, will seek to enter in, and shall not be able. [25] When once the master of the house is risen up, and hath shut to the door, and ye begin to stand without, and to knock at the door, saying, LORD, LORD, open unto us; and HE shall answer and say unto you, I know you not whence ye are: [26] Then shall ye begin to say, We have eaten and drunk in THY presence, and THOU hast taught in our streets. [27] But HE shall say, I tell you, I know you not whence ye are; depart from ME, all ye workers of iniquity. [28] There shall be weeping and gnashing of teeth, when ye shall see Abraham, and Isaac, and Jacob, and all the prophets, in the Kingdom of GOD, and you yourselves thrust out.

2 Timothy 3:4-5: [4] Traitors, heady, high-minded, lovers of pleasures more than lovers of GOD; [5] Having a form of godliness, but denying the power thereof: from such turn away.

Romans 14:12: So then every one of us shall give account of himself to GOD.

Your Days Are Numbered!

The LORD's Words: "Children, I WANT TO BE VOCAL AND EXPRESSIVE: YOUR DAYS ARE NUMBERED!"

The LORD's Words for Today (Posted at www.End-Times-Prophecy.Com)

Words of the LORD:

"Children, I WANT TO BE VOCAL AND EXPRESSIVE: YOUR DAYS ARE NUMBERED!"

(Words Received from Our LORD by Susan, September 20, 2012)

Daughter, write down these Words:

Children, your LORD is returning soon. So many do not subscribe to this belief. There will be very many left behind—so many left to face destruction and disaster. Many will go straight to hell without any hope of reprisal. They will reject ME to the point of no return. This is a picture of the unwise and lost: those who refuse to believe MY Book, MY Words, MY messengers, MY Truth, and WHO I, GOD stand for. These people will find themselves in the Lake of Fire for all eternity because of their disbelief and their refusal to repent and to seek MY Salvation.

MY Salvation is readily available now, but many will miss their window of opportunity, their chance to seize salvation before it is too late.

I pine in grief over those lost children, to see MY children throw their lives away and trade life and beauty for death and torment for eternity is not easy for ME to look upon. I will uphold MY Truth and no man can alter the Truth of GOD: it is unchanging. If you do not seek MY Blood Covering and the Salvation I make available to you, then I cannot bring you into the Kingdom.

Tears flow down MY Face over MY lost children—those who are stubborn, stiff-necked, and refuse to surrender their lives over to ME for the Salvation I give that is readily available. Wholeness and heart-healing is available for the asking, yet MY children flee into the enemy's arms and find death and destruction.

This is where they go if they don't come to ME. Follow ME and I will give you the love you have been missing: I long to bring you into MY Wholeness and Reparation. This is MY greatest desire to save MY children and bring them home with ME when I come to save MY bride from the darkness that is riding over the earth.

Children, I WANT TO BE VOCAL AND EXPRESSIVE: YOUR DAYS ARE NUMBERED!

You can either come with ME out to safety, or stay behind and see sudden destruction, or the worst tribulation ever known to mankind. Why do you want to buy so much trouble for yourself when I offer you a passageway to safety? I am strong to deliver. Those who are coming with ME will find joy and happiness.

Don't deny yourself this Great Treasure. I paid the price for this gift. I died in a way that men don't comprehend:

I was brutalized for your freedom…

I was struck for your salvation…

I was spit on for your redemption…

I was scourged for your healing…

I was scorned for your sanctification…

All this was MY Gift to mankind. It was thorough and complete. There is no other salvation available to mankind—only MY Blood can bring you deliverance. MY Blood alone will point you to the narrow path—the thin vein that flows into heaven: MY Eternal Rest for those who believe and surrender.

Come quickly to the end of yourself. Let ME Purify your soul by the filling of MY SPIRIT. You must turn and follow ME. I am your ONLY HOPE! I am THE SOLUTION to all that troubles mankind.

I AM THE ANSWER: THE WAY…THE TRUTH…THE LIFE…

Luke 17:34: I tell you, in that night there shall be two men in one bed; the one shall be taken, and the other shall be left.

1 Thessalonians 5:3: For when they shall say, Peace and safety; then sudden destruction cometh upon them, as travail upon a woman with child; and they shall not escape.

Revelation 20:15: And whosoever was not found written in the book of life was cast into the lake of fire.

Luke 21:33: Heaven and earth shall pass away: but MY Words shall not pass away.

John 11:35: JESUS wept.

Luke 19:41-44: And when HE was come near, HE beheld the city, and wept over it,

Luke 22:64: And when they had blindfolded HIM, they struck HIM on the face, and asked HIM, saying, Prophesy, who is it that smote THEE?

John 18:22: And when HE had thus spoken, one of the officers which stood by struck JESUS with the palm of his hand, saying, Answerest THOU the high priest so?

Matthew 26:67-68: [67]Then did they spit in HIS Face, and buffeted HIM; and others smote HIM with the palms of their hands, [68]Saying, Prophesy unto us, THOU CHRIST, who is he that smote THEE?

John 19:1: Then Pilate therefore took JESUS, and scourged HIM.

Luke 23:35: And the people stood beholding. And the rulers also with them derided HIM, saying, HE saved others; let HIM save HIMSELF, if HE be CHRIST, the CHOSEN of GOD.

24. I Can Bring You From Whatever Sin You Have Been Engaging In

Words of the LORD:

The enemy wants to lie to you and tell you, "It's too late—you've gone too far—your sin is too bad."

(Words Received from Our LORD by Susan, September 21, 2012)

Yes MY daughter, I will give you new Words:

Children come and listen to your GOD:

I want you to hear MY Voice. I am pleading for you: I long to come and get you when I come to get MY church. She is beautiful to ME—all dressed in white! I long to take her into MY Arms and carry her away to preserve her from the trouble coming on the earth, to take her from the grasp of the enemy, to save her from the darkness shrouding the earth. To give her the beauty I have prepared for her.

Children, the night is closing in around the earth. Soon she will be consumed by this darkness. I don't want you to stay to face what is coming. I can save you with MY Saving Grace. MY Salvation is complete.

I can bring you from whatever sin you have been engaging in, from whatever trouble has been consuming you. I can deliver you from the worst sin. There is nothing MY Blood cannot cover. MY Blood is Pure and Potent, able to save the most wretched sinner: nothing is too hard for ME, GOD.

I can put you on solid ground with sure footing, clean you up, and bring you into MY Presence. I will take you…just come to ME!

Nothing you have done on this earth can separate us for eternity, that MY Blood cannot cover and make right.

So Come to MY Open Arms. Give ME your sin sickness. Let ME cure your broken heart. Let ME give you MY Healing Salve to see the Truth, to open your eyes. I will bring you with ME when I come for MY church. Your sin past can be covered by MY Blood, the Blood shed on Calvary's Saving Tree.

Why deny yourself this salvation any further? The enemy wants to lie to you and tell you, "It's too late—you've gone too far—your sin is too bad." I stand before you with Arms open wide: ready to receive you into MY Beauty; to clean you up; to set you free; to bring you into hope and love; to shower you with grace and mercy; to prepare you for MY Coming!

I LOVE YOU! Come as you are! There is nothing that MY Blood cannot purify. Repent to ME. Lay your life at MY Feet. I will lift you up to new heights of glory, wholeness, love! This is MY Delight! I want to share eternity with you.

Come, take MY Hand. It was pierced for your transgressions. Hold MY Hand and be made whole. Run quickly. Your time is running out. The future is bright with ME.

I MAKE ALL THINGS NEW!

KING OF GLORY.

YEHUSHUA.

Psalm 24:7: Lift up your heads, O ye gates; and be ye lift up, ye everlasting doors; and the KING of GLORY shall come in.

Revelation 19:7: Let us be glad and rejoice, and give honour to HIM: for the marriage of the LAMB is come, and HIS wife hath made herself ready.

John 6:54: Whoso eateth MY Flesh, and drinketh MY Blood, hath eternal life; and I will raise him up at the last day.

Ephesians 1:7: In whom we have redemption through HIS Blood, the forgiveness of sins, according to the riches of HIS Grace;

Colossians 1:20: And, having made peace through the Blood of HIS Cross, by HIM to reconcile all things unto HIMSELF; by HIM, I say, whether they be things in earth, or things in heaven.

Colossians 1:14: In WHOM we have redemption through HIS Blood, even the forgiveness of sins:

Luke 1:37: For with GOD nothing shall be impossible.

Revelation 3:18: I counsel thee to buy of ME gold tried in the fire, that thou mayest be rich; and white raiment, that thou mayest be clothed, and that the shame of thy nakedness do not appear; and anoint thine eyes with eyesalve, that thou mayest see.

Isaiah 53:5: But HE was wounded for our transgressions, HE was bruised for our iniquities: the chastisement of our peace was upon HIM; and with HIS Stripes we are healed.

Revelation 21:5: And HE that sat upon the throne said, Behold, I make all things new. And HE said unto me, Write: for these words are true and faithful.

Matt. 24:37 states, "For the coming of the Son of Man will be JUST LIKE the days of Noah". Genesis 7:4 states, "FOR AFTER SEVEN

MORE DAYS, I will send rain on the earth forty days and forty nights..." Noah spent a lot of time building the ark, but near the very end he knew quite specifically when the flood was to begin! The coming of the Son of Man is again JUST LIKE the days of Noah!

1 Thess. 4:16 & 17: For the lord himself will descend from heaven with a shout, with the voice of the archangel, and with the trumpet of god; and the dead in christ shall rise first. then we who are alive and remain shall be caught up together with them in the clouds to meet the lord in the air, and thus we shall always be with the lord.

Psalm 12:1: Help, Lord, for the godly man ceases to be, for the faithful disappear from among the sons of men.

1 Thes. 5:1-3 (NKJV): But concerning the times and the seasons, brethren, you have no need that I should write to you. For you yourselves know perfectly that the day of the LORD so comes as a thief in the night. For when they say, "Peace and safety!" then sudden destruction comes upon them, as labor pains upon a pregnant woman. And they shall not escape.'

Prov. 28:26 (NIV): Those who trust in themselves are fools, but those who walk in wisdom are kept safe.

Mark 13:32-33 (NIV): No one knows about that day or hour, not even the angels in heaven, nor the SON, but only the FATHER. Be on guard! Be alert! You do not know when that time will come.

Revelation 20:4 (NIV): I saw thrones on which were seated those who had been given authority to judge. And I saw the souls of those who had been beheaded because of their testimony about JESUS and because of the Word of GOD. They had not worshiped the beast or its image and had not received its mark on their foreheads or their hands.

Sat, 29 Sep 2012

The LORD's Words: "I cannot have people in MY Kingdom who choose and desire evil governing."

The LORD's Words for Today (Posted at www.End-Times-Prophecy.Com)

Dear Faithful Followers of CHRIST:

Today I want to talk about a sensitive subject—just who is going in the near rapture? Well according to what I keep hearing from the LORD: very few are going to be raptured; only a remnant will be raptured; only a handful will be raptured. Someone else who hears from the LORD has heard a "remnant of the remnant" will be raptured and this makes reference to the parable of the Ten Bridesmaids: Matthew 25:1-2: Then shall the kingdom of heaven be likened unto ten virgins, which took their lamps, and went forth to meet the bridegroom. [2]And five of them were wise, and five were foolish. According to the LORD all had a measure of the HOLY SPIRIT, yet only five out of ten were taken—they all had a measure of lamp oil. This is really narrowing the field, so I questioned the LORD about this word and then HE immediately led me to this passage of scripture:

Matthew 7:21-23: [21]Not everyone that saith unto me, LORD, LORD, shall enter into the kingdom of heaven; but he that doeth the will of MY FATHER which is in heaven. [22]Many will say to ME in that day, LORD, LORD, have we not prophesied in THY Name? And in THY Name have cast out devils? And in THY Name done many wonderful works? [23]And then will I profess unto them, I never knew you: depart from ME, ye that work iniquity.

This is when I realized—you can't do wonderful works, cast out devils, or prophesy in the Name of the LORD without the involvement of the HOLY SPIRIT—and yet these guys still were told to depart from the LORD—these were the five virgins with their oil lamps half full shut outside when the LORD returned.

Christians: this is a serious Word and your eligibility for the rapture should be examined. The key to readiness in this passage are these Words: [21]Not everyone that saith unto me, LORD, LORD, shall enter into the kingdom of heaven; but he that doeth the will of MY FATHER which is in heaven. It is whoever does the Will of GOD who is eligible.

Who is in GOD's Will? Those who make a full surrender to the LORD, repent of their sin, forgive everyone, and those who take time to know the LORD. So then, the five virgins with a full oil lamp are so bright with the HOLY SPIRIT filling then they are able to watch for the LORD's Return which is also key for preparation for the rapture. So if you aren't fully surrendered to GOD's Will—dying to your own will and future plans—then you don't have a full oil lamp and you are actually apart from GOD's Will and even working iniquity according to Matthew 7:23. So have you made a full surrender of your will over to GOD, because if your plans for the future are still in place then you are outside the Will of GOD and the idea that the rapture is soon will be nonsense to you and this is the majority of Christians today: the lukewarm-soon-to-be-the-left-behind.

Words of the LORD:

"I cannot have people in MY Kingdom who choose and desire evil governing."

(Words Received from Our LORD by Susan, September 25, 2012)

Yes daughter, Let US Begin:

Today children, I want you to hear MY Words:

I have very serious Words to give you. Children, the hour approaches for MY soon coming. I will lift the veil and those who are ready will walk through. If you are not prepared, than you are not coming.

These are the ones who will not be coming with ME:

All those who are intentionally rebellious; those who engage in witchcraft or the love of it; those who are liars will not enter MY Heavens; those who choose evil instead of their GOD. If you choose evil leaders to have over you in your governing, in your pulpits, when you have a choice to make, I will reject you for MY Kingdom.

I cannot have people in MY Kingdom who choose and desire evil governing. You love the traditions of men more than you love ME. I know the lust you have in your heart for the world—it is an enmity to ME. You cannot love ME and mammon both.

The hour is approaching for MY Return to earth, yet you continue to look back to the world. I am the WAY...the TRUTH...the LIFE. No man comes to MY FATHER except by ME: your MESSIAH, REDEEMER, the SACRIFICED LAMB.

If you choose evil over your GOD, I cannot receive you into MY Kingdom. You do not read MY Book or you would know the importance of the choices you are making. You would know what I require. You would get to know ME.

If you surrender your all to ME and have a filling of MY SPIRIT—a full oil lamp, you would see the lateness of the hour and MY SPIRIT would lead you to all Truth away from evil choices for evil leaders in government and in the pulpits. As it stands, you want to hear what tickles your ears. You want to handle the things of this world and walk with the world.

Your partial commitment to ME is like a dog returning to its vomit. You will be spit out because of your half-hearted love for ME. You will drown like a man, intoxicated, in his own vomit, and you will not see MY Heavenlies.

Harsh Words you say? Read MY Word…get to know ME better. As it is, you have left your FIRST LOVE, the LOVE that brought you into existence, WHO Created you and you were created for MY purposes, not for your own or MY enemy.

The hour is close for MY Return…very few are coming when I call them out of the earth, only a remnant will rise up to take their place with ME in MY Heavenlies. This is written in MY Book if only you would read it for Truth and not to twist it to meet your own desires.

I am a GOD of Truth and soon you will see MY Word come to pass. The hour is shortening. Make time for ME, your GOD. Repent of your sin. Come and surrender your all to ME. Your time is sifting away. Choose not to reject ME. I know who is coming out with ME. Come to ME quickly.

This is your LORD…SAVIOR…REDEEMER…BRIDEGROOM.

Galatians 5:19-20: [19]Now the works of the flesh are manifest, which are these; Adultery, fornication, uncleanness, lasciviousness, [20]Idolatry, witchcraft, hatred, variance, emulations, wrath, strife, seditions, heresies,

2 John 1:9-11: [9]Whosoever transgresseth, and abideth not in the doctrine of CHRIST, hath not GOD. He that abideth in the doctrine of CHRIST, he hath both the FATHER and the SON. [10]If there come any unto you, and bring not this doctrine, receive him not into your house, neither bid him GOD speed: [11]For he that biddeth him GOD speed is partaker of his evil deeds.

1 Corinthians 2:13: Which things also we speak, not in the words which man's wisdom teacheth, but which the HOLY GHOST teacheth; comparing SPIRITUAL things with SPIRITUAL.

James 4:4: Ye adulterers and adulteresses, know ye not that the friendship of the world is enmity with GOD? Whosoever therefore will be a friend of the world is the enemy of GOD.

Matthew 6:24: No man can serve two masters: for either he will hate the one, and love the other; or else he will hold to the one, and despise the other. Ye cannot serve GOD and mammon.

John 6:44: No man can come to me, except the FATHER which hath sent ME draw him: and I will raise him up at the last day.

2 Timothy 4:3 (NASB): For the time will come when they will not endure sound doctrine; but wanting to have their ears tickled, they will accumulate for themselves teachers in accordance to their own desires,

2 Peter 2:21-22: [21]For it had been better for them not to have known the way of righteousness, than, after they have known it, to turn

from the holy commandment delivered unto them. ²²But it is happened unto them according to the true proverb, The dog is turned to his own vomit again; and the sow that was washed to her wallowing in the mire.

Revelation 2:4-5: ⁴Nevertheless I have somewhat against thee, because thou hast left thy FIRST LOVE. ⁵Remember therefore from whence thou art fallen, and repent, and do the first works; or else I will come unto thee quickly, and will remove thy candlestick out of his place, except thou repent.

My Rapture Saints Abstain From The Draw Of The World

Words of the LORD:

"For those who have MY Word and then turn to reject it for the world it is better that you had not been born…"

(Words Received from Our LORD by Susan, September 26, 2012)

Daughter, Let US Begin:

Children, this is your FATHER Speaking. I come to you with a message of Love. I come to you with a message of healing.

The world is crumbling beneath you. It is slowly giving away. Soon the ground will shake and everyone left in the earth will be affected: those who are left behind to face tribulation. There is a group coming out to safety—MY raptured saints…followers…bride. These are peoples set apart, unique from those who will be left. MY rapture saints abstain from the draw of the world, the pull of the lust for evil—rebellion against GOD which comes in many forms.

Even so, MY lukewarm church is asleep. She sleeps though she is warned and will be without excuse at the hour of MY Coming—she will stand speechless when I pull free MY true church, MY bride.

Horror will strike MY lukewarm followers, many of which believe they are ready to leave when I come. Their handling of the world and duplicity of mind makes them unstable in all their ways. They lead themselves astray and those around them. This is no small thing: to lead others astray. It would be better for you if you had a millstone around your neck and you were cast into the sea.

Be careful about the warnings you have been given. Heed them as valuable jewels—for when much is given much is expected and for those who have MY Word and then turn to reject it for the world it is better that you had not been born then to reject your LORD GOD.

I am not to be mocked. Many have mocked ME before and lived to regret it.

Focus your love and life on ME and you will be safe in this life and the next. MY bride is not meant for tribulation: that is the purpose of MY rapture of the church: a bringing out of the people to safety.

Come join these peoples. Reject the world and all that it stands for and I will raise you up and place you in MY Kingdom where there is endless joy, peace, and laughter.

Come join the wedding party! I am returning for a loyal and pure bride. Look to the sky as I emerge with MY angel army.

This Invitation is sealed by the HOLY SPIRIT, WHO says, "COME!"

Revelation 19:7: Let us be glad and rejoice, and give honour to HIM: for the marriage of the LAMB is come, and HIS wife hath made herself ready.

1 John 2:15: Love not the world, neither the things that are in the world. If any man love the world, the love of the FATHER is not in HIM.

1 Thessalonians 5:6: Therefore let us not sleep, as do others; but let us watch and be sober.

Romans 1:20-25: [20]For the invisible things of HIM from the creation of the world are clearly seen, being understood by the things that are made, even HIS eternal power and GODHEAD; so that they are without excuse: [21]Because that, when they knew GOD, they glorified HIM not as GOD, neither were thankful; but became vain in their imaginations, and their foolish heart was darkened. [22]Professing themselves to be wise, they became fools, [23]And changed the glory of the Uncorruptible GOD into an image made like to corruptible man, and to birds, and four-footed beasts, and creeping things. [24]Wherefore GOD also gave them up to uncleanness through the lusts of their own hearts, to dishonour their own bodies between themselves: [25]Who changed the Truth of GOD into a lie, and worshipped and served the creature more than the CREATOR, WHO is blessed forever. Amen.

James 1:8: A double minded man is unstable in all his ways.

Luke 17:1-2: Then said HE unto the disciples, It is impossible but that offences will come: but woe unto him, through whom they come! [2]It were better for him that a millstone were hanged about his neck, and he cast into the sea, than that he should offend one of these little ones.

Galatians 6:7: Be not deceived; GOD is not mocked: for whatsoever a man soweth, that shall he also reap.

1 Thessalonians 4:17: Then we which are alive and remain shall be caught up together with them in the clouds, to meet the LORD in the air: and so shall we ever be with the LORD.

Prepare for the very soon rapture.

Read all the books by Susan Davis:

Left Behind After The Rapture

Rapture or Tribulation

Marriage Supper of the Lamb

Also by Susan Davis and Sabrina De Muynck

I Am Coming, Volume 1

I Am Coming, Volume 2

I Am Coming, Volume 3

I Am Coming, Volume 4

I Am Coming, Volume 5

I Am Coming, Volume 6

Available as paperbacks and kindle ebooks at:
www.amazon.com

Also available for free as ebooks (various formats) at:
www.smashwords.com

Made in the USA
Middletown, DE
20 April 2019